THE GOOD INTERVIEW GUIDE

ROSTERS CAREERS PORTFOLIO

THE GOOD INTERVIEW GUIDE

SUSAN CLEMIE
and
DR JOHN NICHOLSON

ROSTERS LTD

Published by ROSTERS LTD
23 Welbeck St, London, W1M 7PG

© S. Clemie and J. Nicholson 1989
ISBN 1 85631 009 4

Published in UK by ROSTERS
Typset by Busby The Printers Ltd, Exeter
Printed and bound in Great Britain by Cox and Wyman Ltd,
Reading

First edition 1989
Second edition 1991

ROSTERS CAREERS PORTFOLIO

The Right Job For You:
Dr John Nicholson and Susan Clemie (2nd Edition)
£5.95

Your Green Career:
Helen D'Arcy and Gillian Sharp
£5.95

Fresh Start:
Dennis Barker
£5.95

Training For Your Next Career:
Margaret Korving
£4.95

Hours To Suit: A Guide to Part-time, Flexi-time
and Job Sharing.
Anna Alston and Ruth Miller
£4.95

Beat The Exam Trap:
John Korving
£3.95

REVIEWS OF THE FIRST EDITION:

ABOUT THE AUTHORS

After studying psychology at university, former international sprinter Susan Clemie joined John Nicholson Associates where she became a senior consultant. She now works as a training manager for a life assurance company in Edinburgh. Dr John Nicholson is chairman of a leading British human resources consultancy. He taught psychology at the Universities of Oxford and London and has written nine books, four of which had TV series based on them. He is currently working on a new BBC TV series about psychology in business.

ACKNOWLEDGEMENTS

We are grateful to our colleagues Carmen Harris and Hawys Vickery for their assistance and support in the researching and writing of this book. We are also grateful to the Sunday Times for permission to use material drawn from articles by the second author which appeared in that publication.

DEDICATION

For Vera & Len Clemie, with love.

CONTENTS

CHAPTER ONE
WARMING UP

When was the last time you were being interviewed and suddenly thought: what on earth am I doing here? Not because you felt you were giving the wrong answer, but because you were faced with the growing realisation that the job you were being interviewed for was simply not what you wanted. Perhaps you felt unenthusiastic about what the company had to offer and uninspired by the day-to-day requirements of the post. It might have dawned on you that you were over or under-qualified for the work, or that there was simply a bad fit between your expectations and those of the company. Even worse, you might have sensed the interview heading towards a positive conclusion and wondered how you were going to cope with the 'welcome on board' handshake reaching across the table!

Precious resources

The whole process of getting selected for, gearing up to and going through the motions of an interview, involves precious personal resources – time, energy and money. Things that are usually in short supply. It's one thing to be rejected from a potential job you're actually interested in and well suited to, but quite another to put yourself in the position of being turned down for a post that wasn't suited to you in the first place. Apart from the fact that your resources would have been better concentrated elsewhere, it does nothing for your self-confidence. And of course, the "unnecessary waste of valuable resources" argument applies equally to the company interviewing you.

You might view a number of 'no hope' interviews as a way of practicing for "the real thing". But there is only so much you can learn from experiences of this kind, and they can become destructive. The more interviews and rejections you experience the more likely you are to run out of energy and enthusiasm – just at that crucial time when the ideal job turns up.

Of course, this doesn't mean that it's commonplace for people to turn up masochistically at any interview that's going, without a thought to their own requirements or the specifications of the company. But even though you have a general idea of what you're looking for in a job, there's probably still room for improvement in your approach to the pre-interview stages of job-hunting. If you plan your move carefully and work out what your real needs are (as opposed to focussing solely on those of the company) the likelihood is that you'll be applying for the right post, sitting through the right interview, and therefore increasing your chances of finding *the right job*.

Boosting your chances

In this chapter we'll show you how to:

1. recognise your unique assets – skills, experience,

educational qualifications and interests – in order to help you improve or make better use of them.

2. reduce the number of unnecessary disappointments through efficient and scientific assessment of your needs and what you have to offer.

3. increase the chances of your finding a job with values that echo and reinforce your own.

And finally, we'll show you how to use all this information to steer yourself in the direction of the *right interview*, which after all, is a major step towards getting the *right job*.

But before we begin, how about trying your hand at the following Interview IQ Quiz? See how many answers you can come up with now. And when you've finished the book, check through the questions again to see how your knowledge of interviewing has grown.

How much do you really know about interviews?

1. What's the best way to deal with interview nerves?

    ....

2. Name three crucial steps you should take before attending an interview.

    1) ....
    2) ....
    3) ....

3. What do you think are the most important things a company looks for in candidates?

   ....

4. List three damaging mistakes you can make when preparing your CV (Curriculum Vitae).

   1) ....

   2) ....

   3) ....

5. What preparation should you make before phoning to arrange an interview?

   ....

6. Name three dress sense rules for interviews.

   1) ....

   2) ....

   3) ....

7. How long do you have to make a favourable impression on an interviewer?

   ....

8. List **three** things you must always do when you first meet your interviewer.

   1) ....

   2) ....

   3) ....

9. Can you name four messages that your body should be conveying during an interview?

    1) ....

    2) ....

    3) ....

    4) ....

10. What are your two **worst** features as an interview candidate?

    1) ....

    2) ....

Know yourself

Before we address the issue of fitting the right job or career to the right individual, there's a fundamental question you have to ask yourself: Who am I? This isn't as obvious as it sounds. After all, who you are is in part determined by how other people view you. Working out your personal profile also relies on some pretty tough self-appraisal, even self-criticism. Another complicating factor is the changing nature of personality. We aren't who we were yesterday, much less who we were five years ago. It may be difficult but it's worth taking the time to appraise critically all the relevant aspects of your personality. Apart from helping you to identify your personal needs, finding out just who you are will also:

1. boost your self confidence when you realise just how many positive attributes you have to offer,

15

AND

2. allow you to explore areas that could be worked on to improve your overall impression on others.

One useful exercise is to get someone to write down what they consider are the five best and five worst aspects of your personality. They might even welcome the same favour from you. At the same time, write your own list and use this to see how your self-image compares with your friend's perception of you. You might then feel confident enough to lengthen the list. For example,

Are you:

shy?; bossy?; confident?; easy to please?; meticulous?; a ditherer?; methodical?; an organiser?; cautious?; adventurous?; outgoing?; practical?; creative?; a 'carer'?; unafraid to speak your mind?

Do you:

find it easy to plan ahead?; enjoy socialising?; feel ill at ease among strangers?; like 'things' as opposed to people?; enjoy a varied environment?; like responsibility?; work well with others?; like order?; work in chaos?; prefer a steady environment?; find change daunting?; thrive on rational/logical problems?; like to be in charge?; enjoy taking risks?; welcome new challenges?; have a good imagination?; allow yourself to be manipulated by others?

What does your list tell you about yourself? What areas could you develop further? What are your most striking qualities? Perhaps you're at a crossroads in your life and you feel it's time to change those bits you least like about yourself. Maybe you've been in the wrong kind of job for too long and you reckon it's about time you started to recognise and achieve your potential. Or maybe you're simply making strategic moves within the confines of your particular career path. Whatever it is that made you pick up this book, it's as well that you take stock of the entire personal package you have to offer a prospective employer.

If you don't take the time to tune into who you are, you may sell yourself short, or overlook jobs that match your unique combination of skills, experience and qualifications.

Changing yourself

Having decided what sort of person you really are, now's the time to do something about the barriers standing between you and the job of your dreams. Work slowly on aspects of your personality, starting with modest and carefully defined goals.

Many people lack confidence in themselves and feel they are life's wallflowers. If you find socialising difficult, begin by making a conscious effort to join in conversations with other people, first family, and then friends, then branch out to colleagues and even strangers. Read up on what's going on in the world and form some opinions of your own. Make an effort to find out about other people's viewpoints, and more importantly, concentrate on the special and unique qualities **you** have to offer other people. Everyone has a story to tell about themselves – it's just the way you tell it.

Try this quiz to find out whether your approach to life is as confident as it could be. Put a tick in the TRUE column if the statement seems to describe you, and in the FALSE column if it doesn't.

	TRUE	FALSE
1. I rarely worry about making a good impression.	☐	☑ 2
2. Generally, I am very aware of myself.	☑	☐ 2
3. I am concerned about my style of doing things.	☑	☐ 2
4. I am not often the subject of my fantasies.	☑	☐ 0
5. One of the last things I do before I leave the house is look in the mirror.	☑	☐ 2
6. I don't often stop to examine my motives.	☐	☑ 0
7. I don't much care what other people think of me.	☐	☑
8. I sometimes feel that I'm off somewhere watching myself.	☐	☑ 0
9. The good thing about being shy is that it gives you a chance to stand back, observe others and then act more intelligently.	☐	☑ 0

18

10. When I start talking to someone, I always seem to find something to say. □   ☑

For questions 2, 3, 5, 8 and 9, score 2 points for each TRUE answer and zero for every FALSE. For questions 1, 4, 6, 7 and 10 score 2 points for each FALSE and zero for each TRUE. The higher your score, the more shy you are. A score of 12 or more suggests you are ill-at-ease in the presence of others, and self-conscious even when you are alone. A score of 6 or less indicates that you rarely find other people intimidating, though it may be that you do not find them very interesting either.

Personality pointers

The ability to get along with other people is a very important life skill – and this doesn't just apply when it comes to making the right impression in an interview. If you feel this is an area where *you* need to work on, you could make a start by taking note of the following points:

1. Be friendly – make an effort to smile more and talk to people more often.

2. Try not to overdo the talking though – allow others to have their say.

3. Become a good listener – it's a way of complimenting other people and gaining their respect.

If you feel you need expert help or the support of a

group of people with the same problem, there are courses available to help you change or enhance your personality. Assertiveness training is a good way of learning how to express yourself positively and firmly without resorting to aggression. Social skills courses aim to equip you with all the necessary 'talents' needed to interact with other people. (Both these types of course endeavour to 'bring you out of yourself'). Meditation or relaxation exercises on the other hand, can help in a different way – if you're a more stressed or 'hyper' personality, they'll teach you to slow down and focus inwards.

The range of self-help groups is enormous. And the number of paperbacks available on the subject is growing. Research and explore techniques that might help improve your overall perception of yourself. The end result will be a boost to your confidence. This will be borne out when you're confronted by an interviewer and will also improve your performance in future jobs.

Expanding your skills

Maybe you feel pretty happy the way you are. But are you sure you have nothing left to learn? One thing that everyone needs to work on is technical skills. It is vital in this techno-environment that we live in, to have at least some basic technical knowledge. Most offices now have a photocopier, and phone systems, and an ever-increasing number have Fax machines and word processors. If you're behind-the-times or suffering from that late 20th century disease – technophobia – you could be putting yourself at a distinct disadvantage on the job-hunting front. Now's the time to change your attitude and recognise that technology is here to stay. If you're a typist, for example, be prepared to go on a word processing course if a prospective employer asks you. If you can afford it, invest in a crash course yourself. If you're already in employment and thinking of moving on, make the most of your present situation by showing an interest in the office technology. And if you really are a technophobic, remember that there *are* ways of overcoming those irrational fears of technology:

First of all, list ten domestic, industrial or office appliances. Write down all their positive effects. For example, a two minute meal in a microwave oven is surely more desirable than slaving over a hot stove for an hour. Also, there are obvious advantages to working on an electric typewriter compared to a manual, and even more when you compare both of these machines to a word processor which really cuts down on the drudgery.

Secondly, examine your irrational fears. The most common are that:

a) *machines will take over* – not true. Human input will always be necessary. In addition, research shows that technology has increased rather than decreased the numbers in work, the change is more in the *nature* of work being done.

b) *machines are less reliable/trustworthy* – not true. Machines don't have a life of their own and are only as good as the person operating them. To get the most out of any machine, you must be prepared to make an effort and learn its functions.

c) *machines are too complicated* – not true. We can all achieve mastery over machines. One of the prime concerns of technical manufacturers is to create a product that is 'friendly' to the user. Unless you're an expert, you should have little to do with the technical wizardry and complicated bits hidden from view.

Identifying your strengths

Another step towards self-realisation is asking yourself what your real talents are. These could include 'natural' inclinations as well as the more obvious skills learned through practice, education and experience. People often overlook their greatest talents, regarding them as mundane or routine. You might not think that being good with people is worthy of consideration. But in a service oriented society, the ability to deal with people is a very valuable attribute.

When we're good at something we're also quite hard on ourselves, comparing ourselves unfavourably with people with similar skills but in altogether different leagues. On the other hand, we also recognise that being good at something can generate rewards from other people in the form of praise, approval, respect, even friendship. This boosts our self-esteem and in order to get more rewards, we work even harder at trying to get better. Unfortunately, this could also lead to us neglecting other, equally important, skills that we've not quite mastered. There may be many things which you could be good at, with a little bit more practice. Often though, we prefer to concentrate on those areas that we consider 'a doddle'.

One way of pinpointing your skills is to look at the kind of pursuits you enjoy in your spare time. In this age of leisure we all have some hobby, pastime or sporting activity that keeps us occupied outside of work. They can be the source of vital clues to your personal strengths and overall suitability to particular areas of work. It follows therefore, that if some aspects of your work utilise some of the things you get out of your leisure activities, you will enjoy your job much more. And as we spend an inordinate amount of time in work, it's really important that you enjoy what you're doing.

Try this quiz to find out what one type of leisure – your sporting interests – says about the *right job* for you. All you have to do is put a tick against each statement that seems to describe you. Don't spend too long pondering over individual questions, and don't expect them to describe you perfectly. Avoid the temptation to answer according to what you think you *ought* to be like rather than what you actually *are* like! There are no right or wrong answers, and anyway, you'll be the only person who knows what you have written.

1. I'd love to do a parachute jump. ☐

2. I don't like telling other people what to do. ☑

3. I prefer spending time on my own, rather than being in a crowd. ☑

4. I find it easy to set myself plans and objectives. ☐

5. I find it difficult to make decisions. ☑

6. I find it difficult to get to know new people. ☑

7. I'd love to travel abroad. ☐

8. I think that my friends find me a bit bossy ☐
sometimes.

9. I like to have the advice and support of people ☑
more experienced than myself.

10. I don't like volunteering opinions, in case they ☐
are unpopular.

11. I like to try new approaches to old problems. ☐

12. I would prefer being team captain to just being ☐
one of the team.

13. I blush easily. ☑

14. I don't mind where I go with my friends, as ☐
long as they're happy.

15. I like to wear the latest fashions. ☐

16. I like to be fully responsible for anything ☐
that I do.

Your answers give you clues as to your suitability (or otherwise) for certain types of work. Let's label the personality characteristics A to D. Each one is 'tapped' by four questions, as follows:

Personality Characteristics	Questions
A	1, 7, 11, 15
B	2, 5, 9, 14
C	3, 6, 10, 13
D	4, 8, 12, 16

Count how many questions you've ticked for each characteristic. A score of 3 or 4 indicates that the characteristics in question plays an important part in your personality make-up, and you should certainly take it into account when you are job hunting. Now let's see what each of these characteristics involves.

Characteristic A: Three or more As makes you the adventurous type. You like the thrill of new challenges, and enjoy taking risks. City dealing rooms might be the place for you, or some other area where they value entrepreneurial flair.

Characteristic B: Three or more Bs suggest that you are a follower. You don't like having responsibility for other people, and you would rather implement other peoples' plans than develop your own. You're an excellent person to have in a team, as you work well with others. You would probably flourish in the armed forces, or in the Civil Service, perhaps.

Characteristic C: Three or more Cs means you're the shy type. You find it difficult to mix with new people as you're not confident of your own abilities. You'd probably be best suited to a job in which you didn't come face to face with lots of new people every day, e.g. as a researcher or librarian.

Characteristic D: If you ticked three or more Ds, you're likely to be a leader. You are confident in your abilities and you like to be in charge. You'd be well suited to managerial posts, and jobs which involve selling.

Another way of discovering what your leisure interests say about the kind of job you should be in, is to classify them under the following headings:

1. **Sociable:** clubs, non-solitary sports, drama, etc.

   We vary in the extent to which we need contact with other people. If your hobbies involve lots of contact then you might be interested in areas such as community work, reception work, PA work.

2. **Intellectual:** computing, reading, bridge

   If your pastimes encompass a lot of brain stimulation and a penchant for processing information then work in research, marketing or computer programming might interest you.

3. **Practical:** mending cars, DIY, stamp collecting

   Your hobbies may exclude people to a great extent and instead involve using *things*. In this case, you might like to consider careers like carpentry, window dressing or gardening

4. **Creative:** painting, carpentry, playing musical instruments

   If you feel the need to exploit a 'natural' talent which involves *making* things, try jobs in interior decorating, graphic design or cake decoration.

What kind of job?

Whether your penchant is for people, things, or data, the following job categories will help you focus your job search along definite lines:

Administrative/Clerical
Welfare

Sales/Commerce
Outdoor/Physical
Science
Engineering/Construction
Information/Media
Management
Creative
Financial/related
Medical/related
Legal
Computers
Education
Services
Travel/Tourism

Study them and decide which area/s interest you the most. In another of our books, 'The Right Job for You', we provide more details about what each job category entails. For now, remember that the list isn't mutually exclusive. It's perfectly possible to be interested in more than one category, and indeed, certain categories go well together. For instance, 'Computers' and 'Education', 'Welfare' and 'Legal' or even 'Creative' and 'Management' could go together. The idea of this exercise is to get a better feel of the areas you can exclude from your job choice. What you'll then be left with is one or two broad areas on which you can focus your interests and research. A word of caution: many jobs sound more glamorous than they actually are. What you must do is realistically appraise every area of work you consider. Send off for brochures and trade journals, read up on subject areas, and visit a job centre and discuss your requirements or concerns with a vocational counsellor.

Your job needs

The next stage in focussing your job-hunting efforts is to ask yourself exactly what you want from a job. Are closeness to home and an adequate salary your only criteria for choosing a job? Have your needs changed over the years and have you taken stock of them? Do you want to forge a new direction for yourself? Could you be more usefully employed than you've been in the past? Focussing on what you *want* allows you to discount those jobs that clearly don't offer you what you *need*.

Here are a few questions to consider:

1. What is it I'm looking for in a job?
2. How much money do I need?
3. What kind of benefits am I interested in?
4. Where will I be in 6 months or 2 years time?
5. Will I end up bored like in my other job?
6. What kind of benefits package can the company offer me?
7. How far am I prepared to travel to work?
8. What do I think about long hours and overtime?
9. Do I like the 'personality' of the company?
10. What sort of people am I liable to be working with?

In short – what are your work values? Draw up a list of your work values and prioritise them under the following headings. This will give you a clearer picture of the kind of expectations you would have of a new job.

1. Security

2. Satisfaction

3. Money

4. Variety

5. Prestige and status

6. Pleasant environment

7. Travel opportunities

8. Good prospects

9. Fringe benefits

10. Social opportunity

Expand the headings and list all your requirements under each one. For example 'fringe benefits' might include a car, house, company pension, luncheon vouchers, insurance scheme, mortgage plan, creche facilities, trade discounts, private health insurance, etc. Which of these would you regard as absolute essentials?

Ideally, you should also be looking for a job that makes the most of your talents. And you should be careful to tailor your needs to the needs of the company. Meeting the requirements of a job doesn't mean that you can't further the skills you already have or develop new ones. Part of the challenge of any job is that it calls upon you to widen your range of skills and as a result, gives you the opportunity to grow both personally and professionally. But if you go into a job without any background knowledge at all, the chances are you'll find it hard to cope with all the demands it makes on you.

Be careful not to emerge from one unhappy/ unsatisfactory experience only to go straight into another. In the past you might have been stuck in a job where, for example, you had to deal with the public and hated it. Or perhaps you were submerged under a mountain of paperwork when what you really wanted was to get out and mingle with the crowds. Some of us are prevented from dragging ourselves out of a rut by a fear that we'll fail. In other words, many people are frightened of taking risks. But in today's rapidly changing business world, being prepared to take risks is no longer regarded as an undesirable characteristic. This is a good time to assess or reassess your entire situation, find out what went wrong in the past, and maybe take a chance or two.

The important thing is to be able to come out of an interview knowing that you have performed to the best of your abiity because you *know* who you are; you're able to identify exactly what your needs are; you're aware of what you can offer; you know what the company has to offer you – and more importantly, you actually *want* the job. All of these factors make it more likely that the interview will be both useful and successful.

CHAPTER TWO
ON YOUR MARKS

'What now?' you ask. 'All this exhausting self-analysis is fair enough, but am I any nearer to getting those all important interviews?' The answer is yes. Think about it. When you picked up this book and started reading, you probably didn't have a clear idea of what sort of job your personality, skills, and interests pointed to. Now you do! That's clearly a step in the direction of *the right interview*.

Though some of your conclusions may not have been too much of a surprise to you, we should also have given you some new ideas to think about. Your next step should be to develop a plan of attack.

Pick your target

First things first – identify your targets. Most people faced with the task of job-hunting confine themselves to scouring the newspapers for suitable posts. It's certainly a good place to start. The competition can sometimes be enormous, however, so you must be prepared to use other sources as well.

Some newspapers run job advertisements on a regular basis, with specific days of the week set aside for particular categories of work such as 'Creative and Media' or 'Science and Technology'. It's a good idea to get to know which paper advertises what, and when. Make a habit of getting The Post on a Wednesday, The Gazette on a Friday, etc. And don't forget to consider the local papers. They often concentrate on nannying or secretarial posts, but they do occasionally carry details of other local jobs.

If you know exactly what sort of job you're after, and it is in a fairly specialised area, it's always worth checking in the trade magazines which cover topics like computing, market research or nursing. Many employers advertise in these magazines before placing a general advertisement in the national press. You may already have a specialist magazine like this on order. If you don't, think about subscribing to one – you may find that you get it that bit earlier than people who pick it up in the shops, and that gives you a flying start on the competition!

Now that we live in an era of high technology, you can even hunt for jobs on your television screen – if you happen to have a PRESTEL or a CEEFAX service. These services usually advertise local jobs. And while we're talking about the media, most radio stations these days have special 'job slots'. Job details are read out on air and listeners are given contact names and phone numbers or addresses – so have pen and paper handy.

It's worth looking into recruitment agencies too. These agencies advertise nationally and locally, and they often deal with jobs which don't get advertised elsewhere. The problem is that these jobs generally get snapped up quickly. Because of this, agencies are usually desperate to get good candidates on to their books, and will probably be eager to invite you along for an interview. That's fine as long as they deal with the types of jobs that interest you, or if the focus of your search is fairly wide.

You could make general enquiries at a few agencies to see whether they have any vacancies which might suit you. When you ring them up, agency staff will collect details of your education, work experience, special skills and so on, and try to match this information to current vacancies in a way that best suits you and the employer they represent. Employers are billed for this service, but it shouldn't cost you anything.

Another very good strategy is to write to employers 'on spec' – i.e. without having seen any vacancies advertised. Many people get jobs this way. You may have missed the appropriate adverts, your letter may arrive just as the company is about to put an advert out, or your skills may impress them so much that they ask you along for an interview.

When you're deciding who to approach 'on spec', there are a number of factors you should consider. You need to know where you'd like to be (geographically), what kind of position you want, and the sort of organisation you'd like to work for. These are the kind of questions you should think about:

1. Where do you want to work?

- Do you have any commitments, like family, friends, a heavily mortgaged home, etc., which need to be taken into consideration?

- If so, how far away from home would you be willing to work?

- If you are willing to 'go where the job is', just how far are you willing to go? Would you consider moving out of the country, for example?

2. What sort of organisation do you want to work for?

- Would you prefer to be a small fish in a big pond, or a big fish in a small pond? Does work in a large multi-national company appeal to you more than work in a five-person company?

- Do you want to work in the private or public sector?

3. What sort of renumeration package are you looking for?

- What motivates you to work? Is a big, fat pay check enough to get you in at 9 a.m. on the dot, or is job satisfaction for you dependent on less mercenary things?

Taking all these factors into account, you should be ready to put together a hit list of the companies you want to approach. There are numerous places you could look for addresses. If you're going for something fairly common, the Yellow Pages is a good place to start. Then there are the classified lists of businesses which are often available in libraries. And most of the specialist magazines publish lists of the top companies in their field fairly regularly, so keep an eye out for them too.

You should enlist the aid of people you know. Draw up a list of everyone who might be able to help you.

Friends, family, past school mates and any business contacts you have, are very good sources of general advice as well as of names and addresses. Some people feel a bit uneasy about asking their friends for help in business matters. This unease is usually based on the misconception that using a contact means actually asking them for a job – in other words, it's tantamount to begging! In fact, what you're actually doing is making the most of them as a source of advice, information and ideas. They'll usually be very flattered that you consider them worth asking and be delighted to give you advice or to refer you to someone else who can.

Once you've got your list of addresses in front of you, it is always a good idea to ring round the companies concerned to get a contact name to address your enquiries to. In bigger companies ask for the name of their Personnel Manager. In companies which are too small to have a Personnel Department, go straight to the top and write to the Managing Director.

There are problems with this approach. For example, Managing Directors usually don't open their own mail, so your letter may be diverted before it reaches its target. And they may be out of the country for long periods at a time. But as long as you don't expect a quick reply, your letter has a much better chance of not being lost in the system if you target it in this way.

While it's always worth approaching companies 'on spec' – good things can come of it – don't go in with huge expectations. As an optimistic rule of thumb, out of 20 speculative letters, expect 12 'no thank you's', 6 non replies and perhaps 2 interviews.

Covering letter

Whether you're applying for a specific job you've seen advertised, or you're sending a letter 'on spec', you'll probably need to send a covering letter and a Curriculum Vitae. Let's deal with the covering letter first. The letter below is an example of how NOT to write a covering letter. Can **you** see any points which could act against this individual?

Mr I J Paterson
Crumbling and Associates
23 West Way
Edinburgh

Dear Mr Paterson.

Just a quick note to ask you if you have any jobs going in your company at the moment. As you can see I am a trainee architect with 3 years experience as a sales rep in the retail field. I think I would have a lot to offer your company. My personality is cheerful, and I tell a good joke! Hope to hear from you shortly

Yours faithfully

Obviously this letter is a bit exaggerated, but all the mistakes it contains are regularly made by people applying for jobs. Let's look at presentation first of all.

It's written on dog-eared and tattered paper. Not only that, it's lined, and obviously pulled straight out of a note book. To compound all this, you can see what looks like a large coffee stain right in the middle of the text. Not a good start! Don't waste your valuable time writing letters on this kind of paper. Invest in some good quality writing paper and matching envelopes – it will be money well spent.

The applicant's writing also leaves a lot to be desired, and the letter slopes upwards at an alarming angle. Many employers like to get hand written letters. It shows that you're writing to them specifically, and not sending off a thousand identical letters to everyone you can think of! However, if you can't write neatly and legibly, typing is by far the best option. You can make references to the particular company to further reassure the reader that they're not receiving a standard copy letter.

You couldn't expect an employer to read this letter, let alone invite the writer along for an interview. Remember that the way your letter looks says something about you as an individual. Think you how **you** would feel if you received a letter like this. What kind of person would you judge it to have come from? Certainly not a conscientious, clever, interesting person who knows how to communicate and how to present themselves. You'd be more likely to form a picture of a rather shoddy, unprofessional, careless, stupid and cocky individual.

Let's just imagine that some eccentric employer was tolerant enough to read the letter. What problems did you spot with its contents? Take another look at it.

*1
Mr I. J. Paterson, -------------- *2
Crumbling and Associates,
23 West Way,
Edinburgh.

Dear Mr Paterson,
-------------------------------- *3
Just a quick note to ask you if you have any jobs going in your cop *4 (word crossed out) company at the moment. As you can see, *5 I am a trainee archytect *6, with 3 years experience as a sales rep in the retail field. I think I would have a lot to offer your company *7. My personality is cheerful, and I tell a good joke! *8

Hope to hear from you shortly,

Yours faithfully, *9

Point number one – where's the date and the writer's name and address? Unless you're organised enough to have your own headed notepaper, you must always write you name and address on every letter you send out. As to how you lay your letter out, conventions vary. In the example on page 41, we've used what is known as the semi-blocked style. The idea is that the page should look balanced rather than lop-sided.

The second point to note is that there is no mention of Mr John Smith's title. Remember what we said about the benefits of targeting your letter as specifically as possible?

Thirdly, the tone of the opening sentence is too flippant. Employers are a ·fickle lot, it is true. And what impresses one won't necessarily impress another. But if you're writing to someone you don't know, it's best to keep it fairly formal. Don't get too tangled up in 'letter-speak', though. A good rule to remember when writing any sort of letter is: don't write anything that you wouldn't actually say face-to-face. If it sounds strange said out loud, then it probably won't look good on paper.

Point number four is an important one. You won't impress prospective employers if you can't even write a short letter without making mistakes. Take your time, and make sure that you get it right. If you make a mistake, start again.

The applicant hasn't made direct reference to his enclosed C.V. He just says 'as you can see' (point number 5). Make things as easy as possible for the reader – when mentioning your Curriculum Vitae, make sure that you make it clear, even referring to the page and subtitle.

Point six is a howler! Spelling mistakes are inexcusable. Proof read your letters carefully. If you're a rotten speller, get someone else to check your letters for you. And if you have made a mistake, rewrite the letter. It may sound time consuming, but sending out letters full of mistakes will impress no-one.

Point seven is that you should always qualify your statements. By that we mean that it's not enough to say that you have a lot to offer the company. Briefly outline how your experience and your personality would be assets to the company. Don't go over the top though. There's a thin line between modesty and cocksureness.

The eighth point is similar to point 3. Don't attempt to win your reader over by being casual and over familiar. They may well have a great sense of humour and enjoy a good joke, but you don't know that. It's certainly not worth taking a chance on it when you are trying to sell yourself.

The final point (number 9) is one of grammar. People often forget the rule with 'Yours faithfully' and 'Yours sincerely'. Use 'Yours faithfully' only when you don't know the name of the person you are writing to, i.e. when you address your letter 'Dear Sir' or 'Dear Madam'. 'Yours sincerely' is used when you do know the name of the person you're writing to, in this case, Mr Paterson.

Let's look at the same letter rewritten, taking all these points of presentation and content into consideration.

Eva Hope,
11 Heol y Byd,
Pont Hiraeth,
Gwent,
Wales CD2 RG7.

32nd March, 1989.

I. J. Paterson, Esq.,
Managing Director,
Crumbling and Associates,
23 West Way,
Edinburgh.
EH9 1HT

Dear Mr Paterson,

I am a graduate of Edinburgh Polytechnic with an honours degree in Architecture. I would like to enquire about the possibility of an interview with you to discuss what I have to offer your company.

I currently work for Bricks and Mortar Ltd, as a trainee architect. But, as you can see from the enclosed Curriculum Vitae, I also have three years experience as a Sales Representative in the field of construction and design. I feel sure that this past experience coupled with the practical nature of my completed traineeship would make me an excellent candidate for a job with your construction company.

I am a conscientious, hard-working person, known for my ability to put clients at ease and to assess their requirements quickly and accurately. I believe I would be an asset to your company.

I look forward to hearing from you.

Yours sincerely,

Eva Hope.

You should think of the covering letter as an extension of yourself. It's probably going to be your first contact with prospective employers, so your aim should be to establish the correct image right from the start. Emphasise those of your characteristics and qualifications which match the type of job you're pursuing. For example, if you're going for a job in the advertising industry, emphasise your creativity, sociability and art degree rather than your sense of humour, way with numbers and ability to read Latin! A covering letter can be a first foot in the door, but only if it is wearing the right shoe!

What if you're replying to an advertisement rather than just making a speculative enquiry? Answering advertisements is a time-consuming business, and there is often a great deal of competition – so it's a good idea not to build your hopes up too much. However, you can get a step ahead of the competition by keeping the following points in mind:

1. Before applying, make sure that you meet all the main requirements of the job, otherwise you'll just be wasting your time. It's a good idea to underline all the skills and qualifications mentioned in the advert, so that when you reply you can demonstrate how good a match you are.

2. Keep a spare copy of your application. You'll need to refer to it later if asked to an interview. And if you haven't received a reply from the advertiser within 3 weeks, you'll be able to send off another copy.

3. Some people send in their applications four or five days after the advert appears – so that it rests

nearer the top of the pile.

4. Send only the information that the advertisement asks for. Often adverts just say 'write for an application form to . . . '. In these cases, it's enough to send a short letter saying that you are interested in the post, and asking them for an application form.

5. Spell any names mentioned in the advert correctly. No-one likes to see their name with an extra 'm' or a missing 'e'.

6. Give details of yourself and your experience, skills and qualifications which are directly relevant to the job concerned.

7. Mention where you saw the job vacancy advertised.

Application forms

Unfortunately, even if you follow all these rules, you'll find that many employers still want you to fill in an application form. Application forms are a necessary evil. Although they may not be much fun to complete, many firms believe that they assist their selection process and you have no choice but to go along with this view. But if you keep the following rules in mind, you can make the task of filling them in a little more manageable.

1. Make sure you return the form promptly, preferably within two or three days of receiving it. Employers won't be very impressed if you wait two weeks before replying and you may even find that

you've missed your chance altogether!

2. Remember that application forms have a similar purpose to covering letters. They are a way of selling yourself to an interviewer before you go along for the interview. It will almost certainly be used as a structure for the interview itself, so you must make a good job of it. If it is filled in badly, you won't even get an interview in the first place.

3. Before you begin, make sure that you have read and understood any accompanying notes and instructions.

4. Take a couple of copies of the form. Think about layout and spacing as well as content. Your form should look as attractive to the reader as possible. Check spelling and grammar on the rough copy and copy the final version on to the form only when you are completely happy with it.

5. Tell the truth, but not necessarily the whole truth. For example, if asked the reason why you're looking for another job, don't say 'redundancy', say 'career advancement'!

6. Be brief and to the point. Employers won't want to wade through a lot of waffle.

7. If there is a space for 'Hobbies and Pastimes', use it to show yourself in a favourable light. In other words, try to convey the image of an active personality. But be careful not to overdo it. You don't want to give the impression of a life so crammed with leisure interests that there's no time left for work!

8. If you're given the chance to expand under 'Further Information', reiterate your main marketable qualities as set out in your C.V.

9. Since you'll probably have to answer questions about your application form in any interviews you get, it's a good idea to keep a copy for yourself. Then you can make sure you're familiar with all your answers before the day.

Even when the employer doesn't ask for a C.V., you should try to include one. Application forms are not always laid out in a way that allows you to show yourself in a good light. Refer to your C.V. on the form and then staple the two together.

Curriculum Vitae

Whether you're replying to an advertisement, or applying 'on spec', your C.V. also has to be very carefully put together. It's not as painful as it sounds either! A Curriculum Vitae, or C.V. for short, is basically a summary of 'the story so far'. It's a sort of marketing document, which needs to make a big impact on prospective employers.

The important thing to remember is that the people who'll be reading it are likely to be harassed and overworked. And the last thing they'll want to do is read through reams of background information, such as the day you cut your first tooth, or what badges you got in the Scouts. Research shows that employers read and make an initial assessment of C.V.s in between 15-25 seconds! So unless your C.V. stands out from the rest of the pile, it's likely to be discarded rather quickly.

There are a number of ways in which you can make your C.V. just that little bit special. Start off with a bang, by highlighting your main selling points in a clear, concise and snappy way, rather than by listing your personal details or educational history. Try to stick to two pages of text at the most. To give you some idea of the kind of things you should include, take a look at the example below:

Curriculum Vitae

NAME: Eva Hope

AGE: 27 (d.o.b. 1.1.62)

HOME ADDRESS: 11 Heol y Byd
                    Pont Hiraeth
                    Gwent
                    Wales
                    CD2 RJ7

MARITAL STATUS: Single

EDUCATION: 1973-78   Southway Comprehensive School,
                              Caerleon, Gwent

                    1978-80   Anodd Sixth Form College,
                              Newport, Gwent

                    1980-83   Edinburgh Polytechnic

QUALIFICATIONS: *GCE 'O' levels June 1978*:

                    English Lit. (A); English Lang. (B); Maths (A); Woodwork (A); Chemistry (A); French (B); Physics (A); Art (A)

                    GCE 'A' levels June 1980:

                    Art (A); Technical Drawing (A); Maths (B)

                    BA (Hons) 1st Class: Architecture

                    Driving Licence

46

ACTIVITIES AND INTERESTS	*School*:	Hockey and swimming teams; ran school tuck shop; piano (Grade 5)
	College:	Elected to Student Representative Council; swimming team
	University:	Treasurer – Student Union
	General:	Hill walking, swimming, scuba diving, camping, DIY

I am generally an 'outdoor' person. I enjoy travelling and meeting people and I am part of a group of volunteers who once monthly take disabled and old folk on outings to scenic rural locations

WORK EXPERIENCE	*1977-80*:	Saturday sales assistant, Harrison Hardware, Shopping City, Cwmbran.
	Summer '81:	6 weeks casual employment, Department of Transport Road Traffic Survey
	1983-86:	Sales Representative Jonathan Arbuckle, Shopfitting Designs.

My responsibilities were to have a sound technical knowledge of the product (commercial designs of specialised steel structures); keeping up to date by reading the trade press; identifying new customers and targeting them

| | *1986-Present*: | Trainee Architect Bricks & Mortar Ltd, Paramount Industrial Estate, Pont Hiraeth, Gwent, Wales. |

My duties (under supervision) include consulting with clients on such factors as type, style and cost limitation of proposed buildings. Arranging site surveys, presenting site plans and submitting these to the client and local authority for approval; checking progress on-site and ensuring that all contract specifications are met.

Referees: Professor C. Ment	Mr P. Harrison
Dept. of Architecture	Harrison Hardware
Edinburgh Polytechnic	Shopping City
Scotland	Cwmbran
	Wales

The main aim of a C.V. is to give prospective employers an impression of your achievements, education, qualifications, experience and personality, that makes them keen to give you an interview.

Ideally it should be typed rather than hand-written. It's quite a good idea to leave a space at the top to enter the job title and the name of the company to which you are applying.

Some people prefer to present their histories in chronological order, while others prefer to start with their current situation and work backwards. Both methods are perfectly valid. However, if an advertisement asks for a chronological C.V., you should send just that, even if it means rethinking your standard one.

If you decide to include referees' names and addresses in your C.V., to allow prospective employers to check your credentials, make sure you get their permission first. It could be rather embarrassing for you if one of your referees refused to give information to a prospective employer.

And if this all sounds like rather hard work, there are firms who specialise in putting together C.V.s. They usually advertise in the up-market press. They can be quite pricey, though, so ask what their fees are before you commit yourself.

Nowadays, it is also possible to get ready printed C.V.s. These are basically standard application forms, with spaces for you to fill in all your details. They usually tear out of a book, and have stubs on which you fill in details of who you sent it to, and when.

Telephone manner

One last thought about applying for jobs. Occasionally, job advertisements give you a number to ring for more information. If this happens, it is best to be prepared to answer a few questions yourself, as employers often use this as an initial screening stage. So it's a good idea to have thought a little about the post being advertised before you call. Be prepared to answer such questions as 'why do you feel you are suited to this job?' and 'what skills do you have to offer us?'.

If you're calling from a pay phone, make sure you have enough money for a fairly long 'phone call, or better still, use a 'phone card. Make sure that you know the name of the person you are calling (if one was given in the advert) and if you don't, ask for the personnel department. Remember to jot down the name of whoever you talk to, as you may need to call again.

If you are ringing for more information about the job, have a checklist handy of all the questions you want to ask. If you don't, they will disappear out of your head as soon as the prospective employer picks up the 'phone.

Have a pencil and paper ready so that you can jot down any information you're given. And before you hang up, check that you have all the details you need, and that they are correct.

Selling yourself

By following all the rules set out above, you can greatly increase the chance that your letters will lead to offers of interviews. But what if you don't come up trumps on a job you feel you are particularly suited for? Or put another way, once rejected – is that it? The answer is 'not necessarily'. That begs the question 'How far should I go to convince prospective employers that I am the ideal candidate for the job?'

The legend of the graduate who desperately wanted to get into advertising comes to mind here. Having failed to get himself any interviews, he wrote a sales brochure describing his background, achievements and personality, added a photograph of himself in fancy dress, and went round all the major advertising agencies handing out copies to everyone going in and out! It got nowhere with the first six agencies he tried, who thought he was a bit crazy to try such a stunt. However, his persistence and originality impressed the

Creative Director of the seventh company. He granted our enterprising friend an interview, and eventually – a job.

You shouldn't have to go quite this far. But if you really feel that you are perfect for a job, persistence can often pay off. If you don't hear from the company concerned, or if they write telling you that they won't be offering you an interview, call them and ask to speak to the individual who signed the letter. Explain that you feel you have a lot to offer them – and why.

If you find the thought of selling yourself over the 'phone intimidating, try writing again. Make sure you send some fresh material, though. If you sent a short covering letter and a copy of your C.V. first time round, try a longer in-depth letter this time.

If neither of these tactics prove fruitful, you'll just have to put the job in the category of 'The ones that got away'. Try not to get too despondent, think of it as the company's loss rather than your own.

Let's suppose you've followed all our hints and sent off an imaginatively constructed and immaculately presented C.V., together with some scintillating cover letters. Or perhaps your telephone manner has convinced someone you were worth taking a look at. Either way, the offers of interviews are now flooding in. Unfortunately, there's no time for relaxation. There's still quite a lot of work to be done before the interview arrives. In the next chapter we'll take a look at the preparation period.

CHAPTER THREE
GET SET

The more you arm yourself with facts about the job you've applied for and the company you've applied to, the more impressive you'll be at your interview. So as soon as you're given an interview date, you should start doing the necessary research.

If the company concerned is fairly large, start by ringing their head office and asking for their current Annual Report. This should tell you something about the company's outlook and prospects, as well as arming you with facts and figures about profitability and turnover. Having this sort of information at your fingertips is bound to score points with any interviewer.

Alternatively, you could call at the company's offices in person and collect as many brochures, company magazines and catalogues as you can lay your hands on. You'll often find these lying around the reception area. This visit will also give you the chance to find out how long it takes to get to the offices, and you can have a look around and assess the work environment. You might also like to check what people are wearing, so that you can dress appropriately on the big day. More about this later.

Scout around for information outside the company, too. There are a variety of books and directories available at business institutes and public libraries which contain all sorts of practical information about companies, such as number of employees, and location of offices.

Doing your homework

Interviewers often ask candidates towards the end of their interview if they have any questions. Many people think that this is their chance to ask about salary, holidays and bonus payments. In fact, you should try and find these things out before the interview, so that you can concentrate during the interview on asking the kind of positive questions that contribute to your main objective of selling yourself. Interviewers aren't generally impressed by candidates whose main interest seems to be what they're going to earn or how many weeks' holiday they're entitled to!

Make a list of the kind of things you'd like to find out before the interview. It might look something like this:

What is the salary?
Where will I be working?
How will I be paid?
What holiday entitlements will I have?
Will my current holiday plans be honoured?
Will there be any overtime – and will I be paid for it?
Will I be able to travel to work on public transport?
Are there car parking facilities available?
Will I be entitled to a company car?
Is the company well-established – does it offer job security?

Are there canteen facilities?
Will I be provided with luncheon vouchers?
What opportunities for training will I have?
What is the attitude of the company towards study leave?
What are the opportunities for promotion?
When will I be expected to start?

You'll need to be fully conversant with the company – its current position in the market, number of employees, and product range – no matter what job you're going for. If you know next to nothing about the position being offered or indeed about the company itself, it will show up in the conversation and the interviewer will think that you're not really interested in the job. The kind of knowledge you should have at your finger tips includes:

What does the company make/sell?
Where is it located?
How profitable is it?
Is it a market leader?
Who are its customers?
What is its turnover?
How many employees are there?
What is the working environment like?

Once you've found out the answers to these questions, you must devise a way of storing that information in a manageable and easily referred to system. Start your own interview files. Each file should contain all the information you have about the job and the company concerned. If you are responding to an advertisement, staple it to the front of the file. If you're applying speculatively, write 'on spec' on the front. You should also record the date of any interview, and a short summary of any written or verbal contact between you and the company.

Inside the file you should have copies of your letter of application, any application form you had to fill in, correspondence between you and the company, and any notes you've made on the company's background.

Your interview plan

About a week before the interview you should devise an interview plan. This should look something like this:

Name of company: Masters and Jonboy Ltd

Position applied for: Marketing Assistant

Date of Interview: 31st February

Address of
company: 291 Marchmont Avenue,
                Cottering,
                East Wessex

How long it will   1 hour (by train)
take to get to
the interview:

Background   Market leaders in the production of nappies,
Information: and surgical dressings. Turnover of 22 million
                in 1988, profits of 2.5 million.
                Staff of 450

Additional points My technical knowledge will be put to the
to note about the test
interview:

Material I should   Copy of my college certificate
take to the
interview:

Questions I must remember to ask:	Will the company provide financial support for further study? What are my prospects for promotion?
General impressions of the interview:	Job contained more administrative elements than I imagined. Pleasant surroundings, and cheerful atmosphere
Date I can expect to hear the results:	17th March
Result of interview:	Offered further interview (29th March)
Points learned from the interview:	Need to research company background a little more thoroughly next time

Practice run

Once you've got your interview plan, the next stage in your preparation should be to practice answering the kind of questions you might face at the interview. And if you're going to be asked to take any written or oral test, now is the time when you should be brushing up your specialist knowledge and thinking about ways of coping with the test situation.

The kind of questions you're asked will vary enormously. However, there are three you can bet on coming up, time and time again. These are:

'Can you tell me a little bit about yourself?'

'Why do you want to leave your current job?'

'Why do you want this job?'

Think carefully about these questions and formulate

answers in your mind. Remember you are trying to create an image of a dynamic, capable and likeable individual. Don't exaggerate your talents and attributes too much, but do try to present yourself in as positive a light as possible. Don't bad-mouth your current company, as that will merely give interviewers the impression that you are a rather disloyal and untrustworthy character. 'I'm looking to take my career one step further', always sounds better that 'I hate the people at Joe Bloggs and Co.'.

Some companies now use tests as recruitment aids, so it's a good idea to prepare yourself for them. There are two types of test you may encounter. The first type, the personality test, is designed to find out what kind of person you are, or 'what makes you tick'. Most ask you to describe your behaviour, or to imagine how you would behave in certain situations. An example of this sort of question would be:

'You are working in your local supermarket when you see your next door neighbour putting some chocolate into her handbag and leaving the shop without paying. What would you do?'

OR

'How would you deal with sexual harassment from a senior member of staff?'

It's best to answer these questions as honestly as possible, as most of the tests have built-in lie detectors. It's usually very easy to work out the kind of answer the tester is looking for, and it is perfectly acceptable for you to answer accordingly – as long as you're happy to work for a company with the kind of culture that the answer suggests. Remember there are no right and wrong answers in personality tests.

The second type of test is the aptitude test, of which there are several kinds. These are designed to test your level of knowledge or understanding, for example, of numbers, language, mechanics or technology. Make sure you are up-to-date with all the specialist information in your field.

The best way to prepare for these tests is to practice, and many companies send out practice forms with the letter inviting you for an interview. If they don't, there are a number of books that you can buy, such as H.J. Esyenck's 'Know Your Own IQ', which include practice tests.

No matter how much you practice, the actual test situation is bound to make you nervous. Here are some hints on how to cope with test taking:

1. First of all, relax. After all, with all the preparation you have put in, you should have no reason for pessimism!

2. If you can't answer a question, move on. These tests are usually timed, and it's best to try and get as many of the questions answered as possible.

3. Make sure that you answer all the questions. If the test allows you to choose between several options, you might get the answer through chance alone.

Remember that today's psychological tests are very sophisticated, and a lot of research evidence points to them being very effective means of predicting future performance in the jobs concerned. They are usually administered by highly trained and experienced staff who know just how to get the best out of the candidates in front of them.

Some companies are very happy to let you see the results of the tests you've taken, and many offer feedback sessions which combine explanation of results with advice on how to improve performance in the areas tested.

Even if you don't get the job, don't assume that you've failed the tests. Try to remember that tests are designed to put more of the right people in jobs that suit them. You would be miserable in a job which wasn't right for you.

Your anxiety rating

Don't get too anxious about the prospect of being tested. Anxiety will affect your performance, and generally make you feel miserable. Try this questionnaire to discover how much anxiety affects your life at the moment.

Put a tick in the YES column if you agree with the question, and the NO column if you don't. Try and be as honest as possible – after all, you're the only person who will see the answers.

	YES	NO
1. Do you blush more often than most people?	☐	☐

2. Would you say you don't often lose sleep over problems? □ □

3. Are you usually a calm person who is not easily upset? □ □

4. As a child, were you more afraid of the dark than most other children? □ □

5. If you've made an awkward social gaffe, do you usually get over it quite soon? □ □

6. Do you find it difficult to sit still without fidgeting? □ □

7. Do you usually manage to keep your cool when things don't go according to plan? □ □

8. Can you relax easily when sitting or lying down? □ □

9. Do you often wake up sweating after having had a nightmare? □ □

10. Have you ever felt the need to take tranquillisers (eg Valium)? □ □

To score: for questions 1, 4, 6, 9 and 10, score 2 points for each YES answer, and zero for every NO. For questions 2, 3, 5, 7 and 8, score 2 points for each NO and zero for each YES. The higher your score, the more anxious you are. A score of 16 or more suggests that you are very anxious, while a score of 8 or less indicates that you are quite well armoured against anxiety.

Remember that it is perfectly natural to be anxious in the test situation, and indeed before an interview – it's not a sign of inadequacy on your part. When you're anxious, your body produces adrenaline which helps keep you on your toes, and makes you think faster. The problem comes when you stay anxious for long periods of time, and your body produces too much adrenaline. There is a very fine dividing line between being justifiably keyed up and ready to do your best and being rendered helpless with panic. So try not to get worked up about staying calm!

Relaxation techniques

If you do suffer from anxiety, remember that you are not alone. A recent British National Health Survey of Health and Development found that an average of 43% of men and women working full-time suffered from anxiety at some stage in their lives. And what is more, there is something you can do about it. Take some time out each day to relax and gather your strength. There are a number of different relaxation techniques you could try, but here's one to start with. It combines elements of meditation, visualisation and 'progressive muscle relaxation':

1. **Find a quiet place** where you will not be interrupted. (Take the 'phone off the hook, ask people not to disturb you.)

2. **Close your eyes and relax.** Slowly take three deep breaths and visualise each part of your body relaxing progressively from your toes to your head.

3. **Count slowly** from 10 to 1. Visualise yourself descending to a peaceful state of mind, which can be achieved by seeing yourself in a peaceful scene from nature, a hideaway room, or any comfortable place you like.

4. **Slowly repeat the letter 'A'** in your mind. When other thoughts come in, let them pass and gently return to repeating the letter 'A'. It is important to avoid straining to concentrate.

5. **Count yourself back up** from 1 to 10 and say to yourself that you will awake refreshed, relaxed, and in a positive state of mind.

Practice this for 10 to 20 minutes at least once a day, and you should find your anxiety beginning to subside. Try to keep a sense of proportion about the interview. Be positive about yourself and your knowledge. You won't get every job you're interviewed for, but you can make sure you have more chance of getting a job by being properly prepared.

Dressed to win

Now that you're prepared mentally, what about your physical state? What you wear has a huge influence on the impression you make. After all, your clothes can be distinguished at a distance, well before your facial expression or voice tone are clear. In a society in which we make brief social contacts with people everyday, clothes have become the main clue to status and behaviour.

Immediate reactions to strangers are based on the first

impression we get of them. A lot of this impression is based on the clothes the person is wearing at the time. Research shows that interviewers form 90% of their opinion of you within the first 1.5 minutes. You're not going to have time in the interview situation to correct any misconceptions, so it's important to get your attire just right.

The best general rule you can follow when trying to decide what to wear is 'play it safe'. Employers don't like extremes, so don't wear your comfy tracksuit and training shoes – even if you look on them rather fondly as an expression of your personality! At the same time, don't wear your penguin suit and tails, or your gold lamé strapless number. Being dressed completely in one colour from top to toe is also a bad idea, especially if it is a dark colour, as this sends a very negative message.

If you've already been along to the company concerned – on a leaflet run, for example – you might have some idea of the dress etiquette there. If you haven't got that clue to work on, here are some general rules you should follow:

For men:

1. The answer to the clothing riddle for men is almost always a suit (unless you're asked to be 'smart/ casual' in which case a blazer and a pair of smart trousers is perfectly acceptable). Similarly, the only entirely 'safe' colour for shoes is black.

2. Above all, check that your suit is clean and well pressed, with no buttons missing or gaping holes in the seams.

3. Make sure your shirt is clean, and your shoes well polished.

4. Don't be too adventurous on the tie front either. You may be particularly fond of your hand-painted silk tie depicting a naked woman, but the interviewer is unlikely to be impressed – especially if they are female.

For women:

1. Deciding what to wear is much more difficult if you are female, simply because there are so many more possibilities. However, the same general guidelines apply.

2. Unless you feel particularly strongly about it, it's best not to wear trousers, as some employers still find females in trousers unacceptable.

3. Go for a fairly straight-laced outfit, like a suit. Stripes and checks are very business-like and give the impression of efficiency.

4. If your hair is long, tie it neatly back.

5. Don't wear lots of jangly jewellery.

Whether you're male or female, the better groomed you look the more efficient and business-like you'll appear. Taking the trouble to dress carefully is a sign that the job is important to you, and the interviewer will take you more seriously too.

Whatever you decide to wear on the big day, it's very important that you feel comfortable in it. Try on the whole outfit a couple of days before the interview. If you feel something isn't quite right – the trousers are a little too short, or the skirt flaps open at the front – don't wear it. You'll be conscious of it throughout the interview.

Unless money is very tight, try to have at least two or three interview outfits. If you only have one, and you wear it to a few interviews without success, it may become associated in your mind with failure. And you won't have a change of clothing if you're asked along for a second interview. This doesn't mean you have to pay out hundreds of pounds for three new suits. If you're a man, try varying your shirts and ties. And if you're a woman, change the blouse and the tights you wear.

Making your entrance

Finally, don't walk into the interview room carrying your weekly groceries, or the last ten copies of the TV Times. If you can't avoid taking this kind of thing to the interview, leave them outside in reception. The same goes for your winter coat, and your umbrella.

And of course it's not only important that you look the part when you arrive at your interview. It's also crucial that you arrive on time. Aim to report to the receptionist about 15 minutes before your interview is due to start. Punctuality always gives a good impression. And if you have to run half a mile to get there on time, you won't be in your most calm and relaxed frame of mind.

So make sure you know exactly where you're going to

– look the address up on the map to make sure. Decide how you are going to get there, and do a dummy-run about a week before to see how long you should expect the journey to take. If you're going to drive there, remember to take the traffic into account, especially if you're likely to get caught in the rush hour congestion.

If you're late, despite all your careful planning, ring up and explain that you are on your way, but you'll be a bit late. If you're going to be more than 10 minutes late, offer to reschedule the interview. Don't give some long-winded, unlikely sounding excuse either, keep it brief and to the point.

You should now be prepared for any eventuality – excepting a hurricane or earthquake! So let's move on to look at the interview itself.

CHAPTER FOUR
GO!

Your palms are sweating, your face is a ghastly shade of green, and you're convinced you're going to be sick. No, you're not suffering from malaria or typhoid, it's a clear-cut case of 'waiting roomitis'. Don't panic though. It's perfectly natural for you to feel nervous just before an interview, and there are ways of putting your nerves to good use, by doing a bit of amateur detective work.

Spot the clues

First of all, think about how you were treated on arrival. If there was a doorman, did he treat you with respect? Were you told how long you would have to wait? Were you offered coffee or tea? Did the receptionist act as though she was interested in you, or were you an interruption to her social life?

What is the reception area itself like? If it's open-plan, this may be a sign that the company has an equally open policy towards its employees and indeed towards its customers. On the other hand, if the receptionist has an office of her own, and peers out at visitors from behind a glass panel, the company is more likely to be procedure-orientated and status-conscious.

Check out the furnishings in the waiting area. Are they modern and trendy, or are they old-fashioned? A company which has modern furnishings is more likely to be dynamic and forward-looking. Old-fashioned furniture, on the other hand, is rather more typical of a conservative, traditional organisation.

Still on the topic of furniture, is it purely functional, or has someone deliberately gone for the artistic effect? Creative companies, such as those in the design or advertising world, buy furniture that makes a statement about their company. More traditional companies, for example those in manufacturing, characteristically go for the basics – with durability and usefulness as their main requirements.

If you can hear snippets of telephone conversations going on around you, are they mainly to do with business or are they personal? How do people answer the telephone? Do they use their Christian names or their full names? How do they treat customers' calls? All these things are clues as to how the company treats its customers – both internal and external ones.

If after all this amateur analysis, you're still feeling a bit jittery, try doing a bit of positive thinking. Imagine yourself walking into the interview with your head held high, full of confidence and enthusiasm. Then think about yourself answering all the interviewer's questions with skilful precision. It may sound a bit silly, but psychologists have found that 'cognitive rehearsal' (the more scientific term for positive thinking) does actually work. The more you think about being a successful, popular and creative individual, the more likely you are to actually become one!

Finally, if these tactics fail to cure your 'waiting roomitis', try the relaxation exercise we mentioned in Chapter 3. Be warned though, it's a very effective technique, so make sure you don't fall asleep!

First impressions

Now that you've done your Sherlock Holmes act, and are feeling, if not laid-back, then at least quietly confident, you're ready for the moment when you're actually called in for the interview. The crucial thing to remember at this stage is the importance of first impressions. Knock on the door of the interview room, and when you hear a 'come in', enter with a friendly, open smile. If the interviewer offers you their hand, shake it firmly, and if they point to a seat, sit down in it. If there are a couple of chairs, and the interviewer doesn't indicate which is yours, be sure to ask.

Now that you're safely in your chair, let's have a look at how you can expect the interview to proceed. Basically you can divide it into four stages. For simplicity's sake, we'll regard each one as separate and distinct from the other, one leading on to the next. In reality, however, the division between each stage will be rather more blurred and their order will change from one interview to the next.

The first stage is best described as 'Sizing up the Opposition'. For the first few minutes of the interview, both you and the interviewer will be trying to work out what makes the other tick – in fact this phenomenon can be likened to the routine which animals go through when they sniff about to find out if they have encountered either a friend or a foe! This is the point in the interview where, after some introductory small talk about the weather, or the horrific traffic jams, the interviewer is likely to give you some background about the company in general and about the job vacancy in particular.

You can get off to a flying start at this stage just by looking your best. Unfortunately, this doesn't just mean dressing appropriately, though obviously it's a good idea to dress to impress. Research shows that observers think that physically attractive people are more intelligent, more competent in their work, more socially skilled and a great deal more honest than ugly people! Attractive people also find it easier to convince other people of their point of view. On the other hand, fat or unattractive people are seen as less good at working and less suitable for employment. Don't get too despairing though if you need to lose a few pounds, or if you're not generally regarded as a beauty. There are ways to increase your interview appeal.

For women, the answer is fairly straight forward – wear a touch of lipstick! A recent psychological investigation looked at how interviewers assessed 12 women, 6 of whom wore lipstick, and 6 who did not. The six women who were wearing lipstick were rated as being more serious, more conscientious and a great deal more friendly. But what can men do if they don't fancy applying lipstick?

Astonishing though it may seem, the answer could be to grow a beard! Why? Because researchers have recently found that men with beards tend to be seen as more enthusiastic, sincere, generous, strong and outgoing. Quite an impressive list, though the results of a single study may not convince all men to throw away their Gillettes and get growing!

Self-presentation

Since getting your appearance just right is a good way of staying ahead of the rest of the job-hunting pack, it's a good idea to find out how much you care about the way you look. Try filling in the following questionnaire. Study each statement carefully, and put a tick in the YES column if you think the statement describes your behaviour, and in the NO column if it doesn't.

	YES	NO
1. Do you ever come out of a clothing store with more than you went in for?	☐	☐
2. It is your birthday. For a present, would you prefer to receive something for the home or car rather than clothing or cosmetics?	☐	☐
3. Does it usually take you more half an hour to get ready to go to a party?	☐	☐
4. Does it make your day if someone compliments you on your appearance?	☐	☐
5. You are going out to dinner. In your wardrobe is a garment which would look perfect for the occasion but is either a little too warm or not quite warm enough. Do you wear it anyway?	☐	☐

6. Are there any items of clothing for which you enjoy shopping? ☐ ☐

7. Are there any items of clothing for which you do not enjoy shopping? ☐ ☐

8. Do you consider getting your hair cut a chore rather than a pleasure? ☐ ☐

9. Do you buy new clothes only when your old ones wear out? ☐ ☐

10. Do you get dressed up only when it is absolutely necessary? ☐ ☐

11. Walking past a mirror, are you likely to sneak a glance at yourself? ☐ ☐

12. Have you ever got dressed to go out, then changed your mind and put on a completely different outfit? ☐ ☐

13. A relative gives you a present of a tie or a scarf which you don't like. Do you wear it? ☐ ☐

14. On holiday, do you make a point of working on your tan? ☐ ☐

15. If you're choosing a new swimsuit, are you guided more by style than by price and practicality? ☐ ☐

16. Do you have a 'best side', or a particular expression or posture which you make a point of displaying in photographs? ☐ ☐

17. Do you care what your underwear looks like? ☐ ☐

18. Whether you admit it or not, would you enjoy (or enjoy thinking about) going to a fancy dress party in an outfit that leaves all the other guests speechless? ☐ ☐

19. Is there any part of your body which you worry about being ugly? ☐ ☐

20. If you were to go on a diet, would the reason be health rather than appearance? ☐ ☐

Score 1 point for each answer as follows: question 1, YES; 2, NO; 3, YES; 4, YES; 5, YES; 6, YES; 7, NO; 8, NO; 9, NO; 10, NO; 11, YES; 12, YES; 13, NO; 14, YES; 15, YES; 16, YES; 17, YES; 18, YES; 19, YES; 20, NO.

If your score is between 0 and 5, it suggests you really don't give a damn about your appearance. This attitude may be stopping you making a good impression on interviewers, and may also be holding you back in your relationships in general. A score of between 6 and 10 suggest that you have just about enough concern about your appearance to get by, but you are still going into the job-hunting arena with a handicap. 11-15: you have a healthy concern for your appearance, you think carefully about each occasion, and dress appropriately. Finally, if you scored 16-20, some people would say you are too concerned about your appearance, and that you're vain – but don't worry about it unless it is dominating your life. And if it is, try to get it under control.

Over to you

After the initial sizing up stage, most interviews move into the phase known as 'Over to You'. This is normally heralded by the interviewer uttering the immortal words 'Tell me a little bit about yourself'.

Remember to think positively. You're trying to create the image of a responsible, creative, friendly, conscientious individual. And don't just concentrate on your work history. The interviewer will be keen to form a view of you as a whole, so tell them about your passion for butterfly collecting or your life-long interest in steam trains. (It may not be such a good idea to relate your interest in dangerous sports like hang gliding and parachuting. Not many employers want to take on a candidate who's likely to spend 6 months of every year in plaster!)

Keep it fairly brief at first. If the interviewer is looking at their watch, or staring distractedly out of the window, it's probably time to stop! And finish up by asking the interviewer which aspect of what you've said they'd like you to talk about in more detail.

Remember this is the point in the proceedings where the interviewer can sit back and watch you in action. And it's not only what you're saying that will make an impact on them. The gestures you use, the way you sit, and the amount of eye-contact, are all important clues to the type of person you are.

The overall message your body conveys is known as body language. It has several functions. The first is in communicating attitudes and emotions. For example, crossing your arms often means that you are feeling defensive, while head nodding gives the interviewer the impression that you are sympathetic to what you are hearing.

The second function of body language is to support and maintain conversation – 'we speak with our vocal organs, but we converse with our whole bodies'. Opening and closing conversations, turn-taking and interruptions are all negotiated, at least partly, through body language.

Research has shown that if there is a discrepancy between what an individual is actually saying, and the impression their body language is giving, most observers give the body language greater significance. Therefore you should give a little thought to the sort of non-verbal messages your body is sending before you go along to an interview.

Here are a few general rules to keep in mind:

1. Body position
The position of your body can communicate important social signals about whether you're feeling friendly or hostile. Pointing or sitting well forward in your seat are signs of aggression, while smiling and sitting with your arms at your sides will make you seem approachable and receptive.

2. Head nodding and shaking

These gestures have a rather special role to play in conversation. They act as 'reinforcers', rewarding and encouraging the speaker, and, as we mentioned earlier, they also play an important role in regulating speech. Staring blankly at the interviewer will make you seem tense and ill-at-ease. Nodding and shaking your head at the appropriate moments will convey the impression that you are listening. And tilting your head to one side will make you look interested.

3. Facial expression

We use facial expressions to convey what we're thinking, and feeling, often in close conjunction with our speech. You may not feel much like smiling, but try to do so at least once in a while. No-one likes talking to a streak of misery for any length of time.

4. Eyes

Your eyes are the most revealing and accurate of all human communication signals. To build up a good rapport with an interviewer, your eyes should meet theirs 60 to 70 percent of the time. Don't be too self-conscious and deliberate when you're looking at someone, though. We all learn during childhood how too much eye contact can be unacceptable in different circumstances. It's more important to remember not to look at the floor or the ceiling, as this gives the interviewer the distinct impression that you've got something to hide.

As you can see then, body language has an important role to play in any conversation. And it is a particular give-away in the interview situation when your nerves are likely to prevent you monitoring it as effectively as you usually do. Here are some DOs and DON'Ts to keep in mind:

1. DO walk into the interview with a smile.

2. DON'T walk in with your hands in your pockets, this can look insolent or even aggressive.

3. DO shake hands firmly and briefly.

4. DON'T put your hands or fingers over your mouth when you speak. It gives the impression that you're not telling the whole truth.

5. DO point your feet towards the interviewer. It's a sign that you're interested in what he is saying.

6. DON'T point your finger at the interviewer. Your finger acts like a club which you're using to try and beat the person into submission!

7. DO look at the interviewer when you're speaking to him/her.

8. DON'T grip the arms of your chair – it displays a negative attitude.

On the spot

The third stage of the interview can be termed 'On the Spot'. You've given the interviewer a bit of background about yourself, and now they want to find out a bit more about what you have to offer. And the best way to do that is to ask you questions about yourself, your experience, your interests and your qualifications.

Most books discuss this stage in the interview as if the interviewer was a totally detached and objective individual, who always asked the right questions to elicit the right sort of information, in the right way. In this chapter, we too will look on the bright side and give interviewers the benefit of the doubt. In chapter five, however, we'll look at some of the common failings shown by more human interviewers and give you some hints on how to deal with problem questions.

What is the interviewer looking for at this stage? The answer is: 'It depends on the job'. They will be trying to picture you on the job. Can they see you taking over from your manager if he became ill? Will you be able to cope with the pressure of work? Will you fit easily into the existing team?

The specific questions the interviewer asks will vary from interview to interview. But you can still predict which type of questions are likely to come up. Remember that interviewers are unlikely to confine themselves to asking you questions about your work history and academic achievements. So be prepared to answer some more personal and sensitve questions, and to talk about feelings as well as facts.

Before each interview, look through the following questions and think about how you would answer each one, bearing in mind the particular job you're being interviewed for. Don't try to learn answers parrot-fashion. The questions won't be worded in exactly the same way on the day, and you'll be thrown off balance if you've learnt a script off by heart. It is a good idea, however, to practice saying your answers out loud. In fact, try to get members of your family or friends to play the role of interviewer – asking you questions and commenting on your answers.

Questions about your work history

1. What progress have you made in your career to date? Are you happy with it?

Handy Hints:
Try to present your career as a series of developmental stages, each job providing you with the skills and abilities necessary to progress on to the next. Make it sound as though this job is a natural step in your career. And be positive about your reasons for moving from your present job – don't be tempted to criticise your current employers.

2. What did you do in your last job?

Handy Hints:
Here the interviewer is looking to find out two things. Firstly, how far the skills and experience you used in your last job match up to those required in this job. Will the transition from one job to another be straightforward? Will there be any further training requirements? Secondly, how successful were you in your last job? In other words, what calibre of person are you? Your reply should therefore mention not only what you actually did, but also any special skills you acquired, and any promotions or awards you received.

3. What did you like best/least about your last job?

Handy Hints:
Once again, remember that you are trying to present yourself in the best possible light. So try to show the

interviewer how your particular skills and qualifications were utilised and developed in your last job. And when you're talking about what you liked least, talk about things like the lack of real challenges, or the lack of opportunities to develop your skills. In other words, try to show that you're someone who analyses things that are important to them – e.g. their job – but also that you're capable of constructive criticism, not just a whinger!

4. Did you have to work long hours in your last job? Or: Did you have to do a lot of travelling in your last job?

Handy Hints:
By all means formulate your answers to fit the job you're going for. Salespeople have to be more willing to work long hours and to travel the length and breadth of the country. Accountants, on the other hand, probably spend more nights in their own beds. But don't misrepresent the amount of overtime or amount of travel you'd be willing to do. You'll only be miserable once you've actually got the job.

5. Have you done this sort of work before?

Handy Hints:
This is a tricky one if you haven't! So it's the sort of question you should be well prepared for if you're moving into a new field. Describe the most relevant experience you've had and present it in such a way that it sounds directly applicable to the post you're being interviewed for. Also outline the personal qualities you feel you could bring to the job – they may be just as important as experience.

Other questions to think about in this category include:

- Why do you want to work here?

- What kind of person would you choose for this job?

- Are you considering other jobs? How does this one compare?

- What was your previous employer's opinion of you?

- How often were you absent from your last job?

Questions about your personality

1. What are your main strengths/weaknesses?

Handy Hints:
Once again, the key to this question is to think positively. Don't present yourself as some kind of superhuman with no faults. Apart from almost certainly being a lie, it makes you look arrogant and lacking in imagination. Try to tell the interviewer about a weakness which could also be interpreted as a positive sign in your favour, for example 'I tend to get involved in lots of different projects at the same time' or 'I like things to happen quickly'.

2. Tell me about the most difficult decision you ever had to make?

Handy Hints:
Your answer to this question might reveal quite a lot about your value systems, sense of responsibility, commitment, and motivation – so think about it carefully. It's best to describe how you made the

choice between two positive options, such as whether to accept a place on a journalism course, or to work in the newsroom at a local radio station. Explain your choice by referring to training opportunities, promotion prospects, and career progression rather than talking about salaries and holiday entitlement. In other words, this is another opportunity to present yourself as an ambitious, thoughtful, career-minded individual.

3. What are your ambitions for the future?

Handy Hints:
Your aims, in the short term at least, should be compatible with the prospects of the job you're being interviewed for. Try to equate your long-term aims with the growth of the company. Don't be afraid to show that you're ambitious. On the other hand, it is probably a mistake to say you'd like to be sitting in the interviewer's job in 2 years' time. They'll either be insulted that you think it would be that easy to get there, or they'll believe you and feel threatened!

4. What sort of person irritates you most?

Handy Hints:
Here the interviewer will be looking for any signs of intolerance or prejudice on your part. So try something like 'I don't tolerate ignorance or bigotry very well' rather than 'I hate Chelsea fans' or 'I don't like Scotsmen'!

5. Is there anything else I ought to know about you?

Handy Hints:
Many candidates panic when faced with this question

because it's not clear exactly what the interviewer wants. In fact, it's a fairly easy one to answer, as basically anything goes! It's another chance to sell yourself – don't pass it up!

Other questions you might be asked about your personality:

- How do you deal with criticism?

- Which bit of you would you most like to change?

- What are your main likes and dislikes?

- Would you describe yourself as an extrovert or an introvert?

Questions about your interests

1. What do you do in your spare time?

Handy Hints:
How you use your spare time is likely to reveal not only the depth of your interests but also the degree of your intensity. An experienced interviewer will be putting interpretations on how constructively you use your spare time, the standards you set yourself and the levels of your physical and mental energy.

Try to present yourself as someone with a variety of interests. Being interested in sport of some sort usually goes down well. Employers don't like to think that they are taking on someone who is going to keel over with a heart attack after two weeks! And be sure to mention any studying you're doing in your own time, especially if the subject relates to the job you're applying for.

Research shows that both interviewer and candidate are more likely to think that the interview has gone well if they have established a link between themselves. The interviewer is more likely to discover this as they have access to your personal history. But see if you can help them by picking up any clues they give you about their interests, especially when they coincide with yours.

2. What do you read?

Handy Hints:
Don't try to be smart – just saying 'books' won't impress the interviewer. Be more specific, and do try to drop in a few serious tomes. A Jackie Collins book may be fine to relax with, but it doesn't exactly stretch the mind! But it's risky to claim to have read books you know nothing about as you could easily be exposed as a liar/charlatan!

3. Have you had any spare-time jobs?

Handy Hints:
Don't just say 'No'. If you really haven't done any work after school or college, or in the evenings, explain that you fill your freetime learning to scuba dive, or teaching your little brother or sister to swim. If you have had this kind of job, try and show how each job has had a role to play in making you who you are today.

4. Are you interested in politics?

Handy Hints:
A job interview is not the best place to create a political platform. But a general awareness of current

affairs will be seen as a sign of a healthy inquisitive mind. Try to read the newspapers in more detail than normal for a week or so before the interview. This is particularly important if you're going for a job in the Civil Service, as they usually ask candidates questions about the big news stories at the time.

5. What television programmes do you watch?

Handy Hints:
It's probably inadvisable to admit to watching much more than topical, current affairs programmes and other documentaries. We all have prejudices about the kind of people who are addicted to soap operas – even though most of us sneak a look at 'Neighbours' or 'Eastenders' once in a while.

Other things you might be asked about your interests:

• What clubs are you a member of?
• Are you religious?
• What country would you most like to visit?

Biographical questions

1. Are you married? How many children do you have? How much time do you spend with your family?

Handy Hints:
These questions are designed to find out how stable your family life and current relationships are. Both these factors are likely to affect your day-to-day performance on the job. Again, be selective in what you tell the interviewer so as to emphasise the positive rather than the negative aspects. You should also be

aiming to show them that you have the balance between work and family just right – not an easy thing to do since the 'right balance' will vary from job to job and interviewer to interviewer.

2. Tell me a bit about your upbringing.

Handy Hints:
This is the sort of question interviewers often ask younger candidates, as there is less work experience for them to base their impressions on. When you're thinking of an answer, concentrate on demonstrating how you developed such personal qualities as confidence, perseverance, ability to relate to others, etc. Mention words like 'supportive' and 'stable'. And don't dwell on any traumatic experiences you might have had.

3. Did you like school?

Handy Hints:
You should be aiming to demonstrate what a conscientious, receptive, disciplined student you were. You might also like to use this opportunity to point out how early on in life you picked up the good work habits which you still use today!

4. Why have you chopped and changed jobs so much recently?

Handy Hints:
Emphasise that you were trying to gain as wide a range of experience as quickly as possible, but that now you are ready to settle down. Show how each job followed on logically from the last. And explain that you are keen to find exactly the right niche, rather than settling

for any old job.

5. Why have you been in your current job for so long?

Handy Hints:
Emphasise the wide range of experiences you have had within that one job, and of course the fact that you enjoyed the job!

Other biographical questions you might be asked:

- Where were you born?
- Did you move home a lot when you were younger?
- What does your mother/father do?
- Describe your best friends.

Questions about the company and the job

1. What do you think about the company?

Handy Hints:
This is where all your homework pays off! Try to drop in as much background knowledge as you can. Your aim should be to show the interviewer how much working for their particular company interests you.

2. Do you know what we produce/sell/offer?

Handy Hints:
If you don't, you should do! Interviewers will be totally unimpressed by a candidate who knows absolutely nothing about the job or the company they've applied to – and you can't blame them!

3. Do you know anything about the current market trends within this industry?

Handy Hints:
This kind of question is unlikely to pop up if you're going for a job as a canteen supervisor, or a warehouse manager. However, you should be prepared to answer this level of query if you're going for a job in Sales or Marketing. So do your homework!

4. Why do you want this job in particular?

Handy Hints:
It's not enough to say 'because the salary is better'! Try to place the job within the larger context of your career – as the natural progression from your last post. And talk about the unique opportunities/advantages of working for that particular company.

5. Can you tell me why I should employ you rather than any of the other applicants?

Handy Hints:
This is your chance to demonstrate how good a match your interest, personality, achievement, etc., are to the job. Summarise all the points in your favour, rather than criticising other applicants. It's impressive to admit to a couple of apparent drawbacks – so long as you immediately demonstrate that they're more than compensated for by other aspects of your character!

Ground rules

You should now have a clearer idea of the sorts of questions you're likely to encounter in the typical interview. And you should also have formulated some answers. No matter what questions you're asked, though, there are some basic rules which will keep you on the right track:

1. Listen to each question carefully, and make sure that you understand it before you answer. If it isn't clear what the interviewer is asking, just ask them politely to repeat the question.

2. Think before you answer – don't be afraid of silence. A short pause to gather your thoughts is perfectly acceptable.

3. Keep your answers brief, concise and clear. And make sure they are relevant. Take note of the interviewer's body language – it will tell you if you're talking too much!

4. If you're struggling to find an answer, say so. It's much better to say 'I'm sorry, I'm not sure about that' than 'um, er, um'!

5. Try to avoid simple 'Yes' and 'No' answers. Give examples, or expand on the question whenever possible.

6. Be yourself. Remember that interviews are not meant to be interrogations of poor hapless victims by vicious personnel managers. Try to relax!

Depending on the nature of the job you're going for, and on the stage in the selection procedure, the 'On the spot' stage could last anything from 20 to 60 minutes. You'll know it's over when the interviewer starts talking about salaries or the possibility of you coming along to meet another colleague.

Turning the tables

At this point in the interview, the roles are reversed.
Up until now, you have been trying to sell yourself,
and the interviewer has been the 'buyer'. Now the
interviewer is trying to interest *you* in a proposition.
Assume that they have discounted one option – that of
not taking your application any further. You, on the
other hand, still have all your options open and it's
your turn to put the interviewer on the spot.

This stage is known as 'Turning the Tables', because
the interviewer is likely to ask *you* if you have any
questions for *him*. There are two important points you
should remember here.

Firstly, you will be expected to ask questions about the
job and the company. Basic fact-finding questions
about the amount of holidays you'll get and the hours
you'll work should have been answered by your pre-
interview research. It's usually a mistake to bring up
the topic of salary. However, if the interviewer asks
you how much you would expect to be paid, you must
have something to say. Show that you've thought
about the question by mentioning your current salary
and saying that you would like to be paid what you are
worth. You should also try to demonstrate some
realism about money, so don't demand a salary that is
way out of step with industry norms. Finally, you
should show that you're not embarrassed by money-
talk.

The second thing to keep in mind at this stage is that
you should have tried to incorporate some of your
questions into the interview. Don't save them all until
the end. Remember that an interview should be like a

conversation rather than a lecture – a two-way communication process. And if you don't have any questions at the end of the interview, don't struggle to think of some. Just say that you feel everything has been covered to your satisfaction.

Here's a list of the kind of questions you might think about asking during and towards the end of the interview.

1. What will my responsibilities be, and who will I report to?

2. How long has the job been in existence?

3. How did the vacancy arise?

4. Who will I be working with?

5. Can you give me a clearer idea of what the job will involve?

6. When will I be eligible for further training?

7. What is the company's policy regarding . . .

8. What is the economic trend of the industry?

Exit lines

Try to reach some understanding with the interviewer of when you'll hear about the outcome of your interview. Don't let them palm you off with: 'I'll be in touch', or 'We'll let you know'. Point out that you are trying to set up other interviews and you'd like to know as soon as possible whether you should keep time free for further interviews with them. Finally, make a confident exit from the room, shaking the interviewer's hand and thanking them for their time.

It's not over yet, though. The candidate who's really on the ball will spend some time after the interview on 'follow-up' activities. You can learn something constructive from every interview you go to, and a good follow-up procedure will help you do this, even if you don't actually get the job.

Assessing your performance

As soon as you get back home, take out your interview file and head up a page with the date, the company you applied for, and the specific job you were being interviewed for. Then write a few sentences about your general impressions of the company and the job, how you feel the interview progressed, how much the job appealed to you. To help you assess your performance, have a look at the checklist below, and put a tick next to those topics you feel you covered well and a cross next to those in which you feel you didn't do yourself justice.

Interview Checklist

1. Punctuality ☐
2. Appearance ☐
3. Confident entrance ☐
4. Shaking hands ☐
5. Good body language ☐

6. Listened to interviewer ☐

7. Answered questions clearly and succinctly ☐

8. Sold myself ☐

9. Asked questions ☐

10. Demonstrated my knowledge of the company ☐

11. Experience and qualifications well-suited ☐

12. Finished the interview on a positive note ☐

A good way of demonstrating how interested you are in a job, is to send the interviewer a follow-up letter. In it you should do three things. Firstly, you should express your gratitude to the interviewer for his time and consideration. Secondly, confirm your continued interest in the job. And lastly, elaborate on any of your selling points which weren't covered in the interview, or which were only briefly touched upon. If you haven't heard from the interviewer by the time they said you might hear, ring the company and ask for news. It's better to know one way or another. And the interviewer will be impressed by your persistence.

You've now got a pretty clear idea of what to expect at the 'typical interview'. Unfortunately, though, the 'typical interview' doesn't actually exist. After all, interviewers are only human, and things do go wrong. In the next chapter, we're going to take a look at the kind of problem interviews you may come across. We'll also be looking at some of the different forms that interviews can take.

CHAPTER FIVE
UNDERSTANDING THE OPPOSITION

In Chapter Four we worked on the assumption that interviewers generally know what they are talking about – in other words, that they are well trained, capable and fair-minded individuals with a mission to get the right candidate for the right job. In real life, however, about 45% of interviewers are reasonable. The rest are either brilliant – or more often – just not up to scratch.

It's hard to say how widespread bad interviewing is. But unless you get lucky in the first interview you go to, there's a fair chance that you'll encounter a disaster interviewer at some stage in your job-hunt. The bad interviewer comes in many different varieties, and different tactics are necessary for each one. What *you* have to do is to work out the nature of the animal you're dealing with as early in the interview as possible. You can examine their body language, the way they dress, the manner in which they greet you, and the type of questions they ask.

The list of mistakes an interviewer can make is almost endless. Let's take a few of the most common, and put them together to construct five caricatures of the sort we hope you'll never bump into. But in case you do, we'll also suggest some ways of dealing with them.

The first in our Rogues' Gallery is a menace only to women (men may find him an embarrassment, but one they can tolerate for the length of an interview). We call him:

Mr M.C. Pygge

Personality:
Yes, you've guessed it, the women's movement has completely passed this specimen by. If he knows that women now make up nearly half the working population, it's cerainly not something he approves of. In fact, if pressed he'd be only too happy to admit that he reckons he's doing more than his fair bit to stem the tide. He yearns nostalgically for the days when a woman knew her place – the kitchen, nursery or bedroom – and accepted her position in the scheme of things – under the heel of her lord and master.

His mother was probably a long suffering martyr, who stayed tied to the stake of domesticity throughout his upbringing, faithfully ministering to every grazed knee and bruised elbow. Mr Pygge divides women into two categories – 'tarts' and 'mothers'. 'Tarts' are all women who aren't attracted to the joys of motherhood, and 'mothers' are all women who are! His ideal woman is a supportive, home-maker, and he sees career women as posing a threat to the way nature intended the world to be.

Typical questions:
Given the choice, Mr Pygge is unlikely to have invited any women along for an interview. It's quite possible, however, that he wasn't involved in the earlier stages of the selection process. He may merely be standing in

as a last minute replacement for a colleague. The formalities will be brief. Then he'll home in on what he regards as the nitty-gritty – your marital status, and whether or not you have any children.

Winning Tactics:
An interview isn't long enough to change the habits of a life-time. You can't expect to win Mr Pygge round. The most you can hope for is a grudging 'Not too bad for a woman' when he discusses you afterwards. You must just hope that his colleague will know Mr Pygge well enough to realise what this means – that you're a cross between Anita Roddick and Felicity Kendall.

Ms Queen Bee

Personality:
Devastating, devious and deadly! Ms Queen Bee has had to be twice as good as her male contemporaries to get even half as far. She has clawed her way up, often in very male dominated companies, by a combination of charm, quick-thinking and cunning. Because she's had to work so hard to get where she is, she doesn't see why she should make it easy for anyone else to get there – especially another woman. Where her career is concerned, she also has tunnel vision. And it's a quality she respects in others – provided they're not her direct competitors.

Typical questions:
Ms Queen Bee will be interested in how passionately you want the job. She'll also want to find out what your priorities are, and whether you are willing to sacrifice your social and family lives to make it to the top. She'll ask you what your ambitions are, and will

be impressed if you are obviously aiming high. Finally, she's bound to ask you to describe the most difficult experience you've ever had, and what you learnt from it.

Winning Tactics:
What Ms Queen Bee wants to hear about is determination, perserverance and true grit. She hates coy women, and sexist men, whom she eats for breakfast! Queen Bees like being listened to – they don't like people who criticise or contradict them. You'll need to achieve a balance between respect for their achievements, especially if you're a man (Queen Bees aren't immune to flattery); and determination to try and emulate it, if you're a woman.

Mr Stiff-Upper-Lip

Personality:
In his late 50s, early 60s, and dressed in a tweed suit and regimental tie, Mr Stiff-Upper-Lip looks every inch the stereotypical country gentleman. He believes in discipline and hard work, and admires anyone who has come up the hard way. He's probably been in the same job for the last 20 years, a real company man. Now that he's coming up to retirement, he's looking for an easy life.

Typical questions:
He'll be interested to hear about achievements on the academic front, or – better still – on the sports field. You'll score brownie points with Mr Stiff-Upper-Lip if you went to a public school, even though he may not have done. But he's also a great believer in life being what you make of it. He certainly won't hold with

whingers or slackers, so you'll need to adopt the heartiest, most positive tone you can.

Winning Tactics:
Mr Stiff-Upper-Lip rates ability to cooperate as one of the most desirable characteristics in a candidate. So it's a good idea to give examples of your team spirit by mentioning hobbies like rugby and football, or voluntary work if it involves groups of people. He sets a lot of store by first impressions, and will proudly claim that he can tell if the candidate is suitable within the first two minutes of the interview. He will admire people who stick to their principles – people with a mind of their own. However, he also likes candidates to respect their elders – for example, him! And be careful not to display any socialist leanings you may have.

Mrs Smart-Alec

Personality:
This lady has picked up a smattering of psychology and interviewing theory, and now considers herself to be an expert. It's easy to recognise a Mrs Smart-Alec. Watch for the immaculately tailored Jaegar suits, the whiff of Channel No 19, and the carefully studied, knowing look. She likes to present herself as a sophisticated cynic, and to patronise everything that moves. She prides herself on her judgement of character, and on her 'feminine instinct'. A very political animal, Mrs Smart-Alec usually looks for what she calls the 'hidden agenda', or real meaning, behind others' behaviour.

Typical questions:
Most of her questions are designed to provoke you into revealing the 'real' you! Your every remark and gesture will be interpreted as deeply meaningful. Even your jokes will be dissected and analysed for hidden prejudices. Mrs Smart Alec is a great fan of the 'Imagine you're . . .' sort of question, i.e. she'll ask you how you would react in a particular situation. She'll also ask you 'what newspaper do you read?' and then read something of deep significance into your answer.

Winning tactics:
With 'Imagine you're . . .' questions, you're probably best off giving the kind of answer you think that Mrs Smart-Alec is looking for – and usually that's rather more obvious than she'd care to admit! Be careful not to lie though, as the follow-up question may well be designed to catch you out. If you feel the interviewer is really moving into the realms of fantasy with some of her questions, don't shy away from asking her what relevance they have to the job you're going for.

Mr Graduate

Personality:
Two years into his career, Mr Graduate is a committed company man. Colleagues regard him as a high-flier who is getting too big for his boots, and who needs a spell in Personnel to bring him back down to earth. He's been to business school, and will drop business terms into the conversation like confetti. Mr Graduate regards himself as having matured over his two years in the workforce, and doesn't tolerate youthful ideals or immature behaviour. He likes to do things by the

book. No-one in his department dares call personal 'phone calls and free envelopes 'perks of the job' when he's around!

Typical questions:
He'll be interested in finding out all about your family background, and whether it matches his. And he will be impressed if you've already demonstrated some signs of entrepreneurial flair or business acumen – for example by running a fund raising campaign, or by starting your own small business. Most Mr Graduates have little imagination, and base their questions almost exclusively on what you've said on your application form.

Winning tactics:
Play down any failures and emphasise your successes. Don't exhibit too much youthful enthusiam, concentrate on mature and rational thinking. Ask about the possiblility of future training. If you belong to a society devoted to business, it's bound to impress Mr Graduate. So will a subscription to a business magazine. Be careful here, though. Don't pretend to be more knowledgeable than you actually are. Mr Graduate will almost certainly catch you out. And the possibility of encountering a Mr Graduate should stop you ever turning up for an interview without reading all the company literature.

Winning the interview battle

Now you've got a good idea of some of the most threatening species you're likely to encounter in the interviewing room. Don't be disheartened. The great majority of interviewers are nothing like our infamous bunch! And now you know what to look out for, you should be able to handle all but the most obnoxious interviewer! Just keep in mind the following golden rules for dealing with all species of difficult interviewer:

1. Don't tell lies. Even the most useless interviewer has a nose for deception. It's perfectly legitimate for you not to mention things that you feel would hinder your application. But if you're questioned directly about something, it's best to come clean. It's better for the interviewer to end up describing you as honest about your failings rather than suspecting you of dishonesty?

2. You can answer tough questions with tough replies, but don't be irritated into becoming aggressive. If you don't see the relevance of a particular question, ask the interviewer to explain it, rather than saying: "That's a strange thing to ask me!".

3. Don't lose your temper. We're going to be looking at 'stress interviews', where the interviewer is deliberately trying to rile you, later on in this chapter. For now, remember that flying off the handle is never justified. If the interviewer is downright rude, however, and you decide there's no point in carrying on, just say that you don't think the job is right for you, and then leave. But it's *very* unlikely you'll ever find yourself in this situation.

4. If you're asked to answer "Imagine you're . . ." questions, let your answers suggest the type of candidate the interviewer is looking for. It usually isn't very difficult to spot what the 'correct' answer

would be in their eyes.

5. Don't allow yourself to be thrown by difficult questions. Take some time to think about your answers, and if you can't think of a reply – say so.

Unfortunately, it's not only the difficult interviewers that can sometimes cause problems. There are some unusual **interviewing techniques** which require a little extra preparation. The most notorious of these is the stress interview.

Surviving under pressure

Even the most accomplished and apparently sympathetic interviewer may sometimes throw in a difficult question to test how quick your thinking is and how you react under pressure. You'll easily recognise the real stress interviewer though, as they use techniques specifically designed to put you off balance and make you feel uncomfortable. And they will bombard you with difficult questions, often aggressively framed.

This technique is most commonly used in the services and in the world of merchant banking. The main assumption behind this approach is that it forces candidates to reveal more of their real personality than they would normally. Whether or not you agree with this assumption (and more and more experts do not) it's still a fairly common interviewing technique, so it's as well to know what to expect.

The questions you're asked in a stress interview will be blunt and no attempt will be made to spare your feelings. On the contrary, the aim is to make the questions as threatening as possible by concentrating on what they suspect are your sensitive points, weaknesses and past failures. For example: "How did you come to do so badly in Chemistry at university?", or "What makes you think you could contribute anything to an organisation like ours, with a track record like yours?" In this sort of interview, there'll be little or no discussion of your strong points – unless *you* manage to steer the conversation towards them.

It's quite common for a stress interviewer to start the interview off simply by saying something like: "All right, you've got 10 minutes. Sell yourself to me." So think about how you would cope with this in advance. Another trick favoured by stress interviewers is to use silence as a weapon against candidates. Imagine how you'd feel if you've just given a particularly good answer to a difficult question, and were confronted by an interviewer just sitting there, staring blankly at you, apparently not having heard what you said and giving no indication of what happens next.

This is a very old trick, and one often used by journalists to get people to give away more than they want to. If you've nothing more to say, don't feel it's up to you to fill the silence. You might say: "I think I've covered that topic now". Otherwise, well, two can play the blank gaze game.

If you're confronted with a rude, aggressive stress interviewer, you may well want to ask whether you would want to work in the sort of company where that technique is approved of. If you still want the job, however, there are ways of coming out of this situation on top.

Avoid becoming flustered or flippant. And resist the temptation to lose your temper at all costs. The stress interviewer's main aim is to find whether or not you can cope under pressure. Losing your temper will be seen as a sign that you can't – no matter how much you've been provoked.

How hot tempered are you? Do you tend to flare up quite quickly, or does it take a lot of provocation to make you angry? If you do have a bad temper, you're unlikely to come out on top in a stress interview. The questionnaire below is designed to find out just how likely you are to blow up under duress.

Your stress rating

Read each statement carefully. If you think it describes you, or your behaviour, put a tick in the YES column. Put a tick in the NO column if it sounds totally unlike you.

	YES	NO
1. If someone does you a bad turn do you usually manage to ignore it?	☐	☐
2. Do you often grind your teeth consciously or unconsciously?	☐	☐
3. Do you sometimes get so annoyed that you break crockery or throw things around the house?	☐	☐
4. Can you usually manage to be patient?	☐	☐

5. Do you like to play at ducking people when you're having a swim? ☐ ☐

6. Would you rather say you agree with somebody than start an argument? ☐ ☐

7. Have you ever felt you would really like to kill somebody? ☐ ☐

8. Do you think that if someone is rude to you it is best to let it pass? ☐ ☐

9. Do you just laugh when you read the stupid things some politicians say in the newspapers? ☐ ☐

10. Do you often make sarcastic remarks about other people? ☐ ☐

For questions 2, 3, 5, 7, and 10, score 2 points for each YES answer and zero for every NO. For questions 1, 4, 6, and 9, score 2 points for each NO and zero for each YES.

The higher your score, the more aggressive you are. A score of 10 or more suggests you are prone to direct or indirect expressions of aggression, e.g. through temper tantrums or violent arguments. You don't take any nonsense from anyone and have a powerful urge to get revenge on anyone who annoys you. You'll be an easy target for the stress interviewer. If you really want the job concerned, try to control your temper. Take a deep breath and mentally count to ten.

A score of 4 or less indicates you have a gentle, even-tempered disposition and are not drawn towards aggression. Unfortunately you may be so nice that you let the stress interviewer walk all over you. So don't be afraid to stick up for yourself and show some gumption when appropriate.

Beat the panel

Another less threatening but still quite unnerving situation is the panel interview. The panel usually consists of a chairperson, who will control and guide the questioning, and two or more additional members who are there because they have a particular expertise, or an interest in the job concerned. This is a technique most commonly used by the Civil Service and by advertising agencies.

Although good interviewers will do their best to put you at ease, it's quite easy to feel rather intimidated when you're faced with four or five blank faces instead of the one you expected. First of all, don't forget, it's quite natural to feel nervous and unsure in this situation. Don't get worked up about staying calm. Here are some winning strategies to help you cope.

Try to identify the most influential person on the panel. It will usually be the chairman, but keep an eye out for the other interviewers deferring to one individual in particular. There may be a joker on the panel. He may be deliberately trying to put you at ease, or he may just be a joker, but don't be fooled into thinking that he's the influential one, just because he's the noisiest.

Always address your answers to the person who asked you the question, but try to check the influential individual's response as you talk. If there's a pause between questions, look to the Chairman for guidance.

Standing out in a crowd

Some firms prefer group selection methods. This technique is particularly common among large companies and organisations who are looking for highly socially skilled individuals with leadership qualities. And it usually requires candidates getting involved in working with groups of other hopefuls over one or two days. Often the job concerned requires a lot of expensive training, so the company wants to make sure that it choses the right candidate.

Sometimes these selection days will be prefaced the night before by a dinner with the company executives. Officially you are not being judged on these occasions. However, if you get paralytic and have to be carried off to bed, it won't go unnoticed! So be aware of how alcohol affects you and make sure that you stop drinking well before the danger zone. Try to drink wine and a soft drink alternatively, and make each drink last as long as possible.

The key thing to remember about group interviews is that you are meant to be **part of a team**. Don't show off. What will make you stand out is the way you lead the rest of the group, and the way in which you motivate the others to do things. You want to make an impression on the assessor, but not as an insensitive bully who won't let anyone else speak!

Be polite, considerate and firm when dealing with your fellow candidates. You'll make a better impression if

110

you try to shine by your own merits, rather than by trying to make everyone else look bad. Whatever you do, don't put on an act. You may be able to keep it up for an hour or two, but not over a whole day. The mask only has to slip once for people to start wondering what lies underneath – and why you find it necessary to pretend to be someone you're not.

Your social skills rating

The key to success in the group interview situation lies in you being a skillful social operator. You must be able to communicate effectively, to listen carefully, to take command of a situation when appropriate, but also to work as part of a team. Try filling in the questionnaire below to see just how sociable you are.

Read each statement carefully and put a tick in the TRUE column if you thing it is true, and in the FALSE column if you don't.

	TRUE	FALSE
1. No-one's perfect, so you have to make allowances with new people.	☐	☐
2. I generally wait for other people to initiate relationships with me.	☐	☐
3. I'm careful not to judge people too quickly when I first meet them.	☐	☐
4. When I try to start a relationship, I am very afraid of being rejected.	☐	☐

5. I usually find it quite easy to show people that I like them. ☐ ☐

6. I don't know what to say to new people. ☐ ☐

7. I find it a challenge to meet someone new. ☐ ☐

8. I am very fixed in my ways and unwilling to take risks. ☐ ☐

Now add up your score. Give yourself 2 points for each time you answered TRUE to the odd-numbered questions (1, 3, 5 and 7) and 2 points for each time you answered FALSE to the even numbered questions (2, 4, 6 and 8).

The higher your score the better you are at getting on with people. A score of 10 or more suggests you are an accomplished social operator. You should be able to manage the group interview situation with flair and to impress the assessor with your social versatility.

A score of 6 or less indicates you are not at ease with strangers and could find this type of interview rather difficult to deal with. But don't despair. You can increase your sociability rating by keeping these simple rules in mind.

1. Be friendly – if you smile and make an effort to talk to people, they're not going to be so nervous about talking to you.

2. Be a good listener. Don't just switch off when someone else is talking. Listen carefully to what

they are saying and ask questions if it is unclear what they mean. Nod occasionally to show that you understand what they are saying.

3. Don't talk too much. It's good to show that you have something to say, but not to the point where it's difficult to get a word in edgeways.

4. Try to relax and behave naturally. Don't let the artificial nature of the situation put you off. Forget about being noticed and concentrate on the task the group has been set.

5. Be receptive to the non-verbal signals of those around you. If you are able to help out someone who is obviously distressed, or shut up someone who is being a bit too aggressive, you will impress everyone with your sensitivity.

6. Finally, just relax and be yourself.

Conquering fear

This last point is the key to dealing with difficult questions, awkward interviewers and unusual interviewing techniques. Staying calm when you're faced with a Mr M.C. Pygge, or a group of six interviewers is often easier said than done. Sometimes the more you try to stay calm, the more difficult it becomes. However, there are ways of keeping your blood pressure down whatever the situation.

First of all, remember that an interview is basically a conversation between equals. Even if you're going for a very low status job, interviewers are just human beings like yourself. So don't accord them some kind of super-human status. And if you find yourself becoming a little awe-struck just imagine them sitting in their bath, playing with a rubber duck, or running down the High Street stark naked. Not many people can survive Trial by Fantasy!

Keep a sense of proportion. Your nervousness is due to fear. So it stands to reason that if you get rid of the fear, the nervousness will go too. What is the worst thing that could possibly happen? You could freeze and find yourself unable to answer any questions. You might irritate the interviewer, or make some mistake that would rule out any possibility of getting the job. But would that really be the end of the world? However disastrous it may seem to you, the interviewer will have forgotten about it 10 minutes after you've left the room. There are plenty of jobs – and other interviewers – and anyway, what about all the other areas of your life?

One of the most distressing things about nervousness is the way it affects you physically. Your mouth goes dry, your palms begin to sweat, and your heart feels as though it's about to break free from your body. All these symptoms are caused by adrenaline – the substance that the body releases when it is under stress. The function of adrenaline is to get you ready to fight for your life, or to run like mad! All very well in days of old. But in most interviews, a less physical solution to stress is usually required. Try breathing deeply. Holding your breath builds up tension, whereas taking a few controlled breaths will calm you down, relax your muscles and generally put you in a better state to be interviewed.

But by far the best way of making sure that you feel confident about the interview is to be as well prepared as you possibly can be. If you've done your research, practised possible questions, and thought about the kind of questions you'd like to ask, you're well on the way to success. And if things still go badly wrong, you'll be able to comfort yourself with the thought that you did everything in your power to make it otherwise.

Finally, think positively. Doing well in interviews is a skill that has to be acquired. Every interview is good experience, good practice and one step nearer the right job. Be positive about yourself as well. You're as worthwhile as any other candidate – don't forget it!

CHAPTER SIX
SPECIAL CASES

Most of the suggestions we have been making about how to create the right impression in an interview apply regardless of who you are or what the interview is for. However, in addition to the general rules, there are special considerations that you'll need to take into account if you're a first-time job-hunter, or a woman returning to work, for example.

First-time job-hunters

Interviewers who have been properly trained know to attach a great deal of weight to *track-record*. This is sensible, since research shows that the most reliable predictor of how well someone is going to perform in a new job is how they made out in a similar post in the past. But it does make life difficult for the first-time job hunter who, by definition, doesn't seem to have a track record to be judged by!

As a result, if you're applying for your first full-time job, you'll need to work extra-hard to put across positive aspects of yourself which don't relate to previous work-experience – personality, motivation, the thoroughness of your preparation for the interview, etc.. And if the interviewer still seems to be worried by your inexperience, draw their attention to the fact that although you may not have had a full-time job before, you do actually have some work experience. What about those part-time jobs you've had, at weekends or in the holidays? The chances are you *have* already developed some of the essential skills they're looking for: staying-power, reliability, the ability to deal with customers, for example.

You might also consider pointing out – politely, of course – that there is an up-side to your having relatively little experience. It gives them a comparatively blank slate to write on. The fact that you haven't worked for other organizations means that you won't have picked up their bad habits or been instructed in procedures that your new employers would frown on. This will make it easier for them to mould you into doing things their way. In other words, there's a good chance they'll be able to turn your 'rawness' to their advantage – provided they have a half-decent induction programme and are prepared to spend some time training you. The tactic we're recommending here – taking a potential negative and turning it into a positive – is one of the most valuable interview skills you can acquire.

Finally, you can boost your morale with the thought that employers need you at least as much as you need them. Population trends – particularly the declining birth-rate – mean that there's a shortage of young people. Older people – and that includes interviewers – are only too aware that it's going to be people like you who'll be keeping the wheels of industry going in the future. Without you, there won't be sufficient funds in the national kitty to pay their pensions! Small wonder they're so keen to hire the right people.

Graduates

If you're applying for a job from college, you're in a unique position. With luck you'll have the support of a careers service which specialises in placing people with exactly your qualifications into suitable jobs. Students don't always have a very high opinion of this service, but at least it ought to relieve you of some of the more tedious aspects of job-hunting.

Then there's the 'Milk Round'. A lot of big companies find it worth their while to send interviewers to the universities and colleges to talk to students on campus rather than have them spend time travelling to interviews when they should be revising for examinations. To save further time, it's usual for students to be asked to fill in standard application forms, supplied by the University. Most students leave it until their final year before joining the Milk Round. The smart ones have a trial-run the year before, to practise their interview skills and to narrow the field of prospective employers.

Milk Round interviews are usually just preliminary encounters, designed to give both sides a chance to see if they like the look of the other. You'll probably be questioned on fairly general topics, such as family, hobbies and other interests. You may also be asked some "Imagine you're . . . ?" questions, which require you to guess how you would react in certain situations. Remember it's best to use your imagination, and concentrate on presenting yourself as someone worth further investigation. If you can't see an obvious answer, or suspect that you're being led into a trap, "I really don't know the answer to that one – but I'd like the chance to find out!" is a useful let-out.

The good thing about this reply is that it positions you as keen, realistic and confident enough not to feel you have to pretend to know everything. It also counteracts some of the most commonly expressed objections to graduates – particularly by people who didn't have the benefit of higher education themselves. Old stereotypes take a long time to die, so students are still seen in some quarters as arrogant, Ivory Tower wastrels who believe that the world owes them a living. You'd be unlucky to come up against this sort of prejudice in an interviewer – most companies take graduate selection far too seriously – but it doesn't do any harm to prepare for all contingencies!

As a graduate, you may also be able to benefit from the Old Boy/Girl Network. Your interviewer may not have been at the same college as you, but they certainly ought to have a fair bit of experience of judging people with your educational background. In other words, your interview is likely to be intelligent and business-like, rather than one of those embarrassing (and happily very rare) situations where you find you're talking at cross-purposes – to say nothing of daggers-drawn!

The population trends that favour all first-time job-hunters apply particularly to graduates. So does the fact that politicians and businessmen now accept that a shortage of qualified people has replaced strikes and overmanning as the major threat to British industry's ability to compete with its rivals overseas. As a result, graduates are back in favour with employers. You are in a sellers' market, which means that you can safely ask your interviewers questions which are every bit as searching as those they ask you. You would be foolish not to have a list of such questions prepared. After all, the ability to formulate – and then ask – the right question is one of the qualities a wise employer will be looking for in a graduate.

Another quality they will be looking for is a healthy interest in getting on. They expect today's graduate intake to provide the day-after-tomorrow's leaders, so don't be afraid to quiz them about what provision their organisation makes for management training and development, appraisal and career planning, accelerated 'fast-track' promotion for outstanding performers, perhaps even succession planning (the technical term for spotting future leaders and preparing them for life at the top). If you want to get a rough idea of how ambitious *you* are, quickly answer the following questions.

	YES	NO
1. Do you set your aspirations low in order to avoid disappointment?	☐	☐
2. Do you try to do things immediately rather than put them off until later?	☐	☐
3. Do days sometimes go by without your having achieved a thing?	☐	☐
4. Do you find it difficult to enjoy a holiday because you would prefer to be at work?	☐	☐
5. Do you find it difficult to concentrate on an important job when people around you are chatting?	☐	☐

6. Are you inclined to be very envious of the success of other people? ☐ ☐

7. Do you try to enjoy work from day to day rather than struggling to improve your position? ☐ ☐

8. Do you often compare your ability and performance on a job with that of other people? ☐ ☐

9. Would you very much enjoy being 'in the public eye'? ☐ ☐

10. Do you let an escalator carry you along without walking yourself? ☐ ☐

For questions 2, 4, 6, 8 and 9, score 2 points for each YES answer, and zero for every NO. For questions 1, 3, 5, 7 and 10, score 2 points for each NO and zero for each YES.

The higher your score, the more ambitious you are. A score of 12 or more suggests you are hard-working, competitive and keen to improve your social standing. A score of 6 or less indicates that you place little value on competitive performance and may tend towards apathy.

Women returning to work

Some women get very anxious about looking for a job after taking time out to raise a family. The prospect of being interviewed is just one of the things that gives them butterflies in the stomach. If this sounds familiar to you, remember that it's not an entirely rational fear. After all, you're the same woman that you were before the break. There may have been some changes at work since you left, but there's no reason why you shouldn't quickly catch up. Your earlier experience won't have lost its value, and you may well have gained significantly in confidence and organisational ability as a result of your experience as Chief Executive Officer of the family. This may sound an odd way of describing things. But more and more personnel managers now accept that the management skills necessary to run a family can transfer to running a team at work – and they're happy to exploit this discovery.

Nor is there anything unusual about a woman wanting to return to work. Quite the reverse. Only 4% of British women these days decide *not* to return to work after their children are safely ensconced at school. Other people's attitudes towards women who return to work have changed dramatically, too. Ten years ago a prominent Cabinet Minister (now no longer in office) publicly urged women not to return to work. He wanted to make the unemployment figures of the day look less horrific! Today politicians join leaders of industry in begging women to bring their skills and experience back to the workplace where they are sorely needed.

So if you're preparing for your first job interview for some years, you can take heart from the fact that you are not alone – and you're very much wanted! You may notice changes in what is expected of you at work, but many of these changes will be for the better. The status of women in the office hasn't advanced as quickly as some would like, but there are grounds for optimism. At the level of middle management, for example, the earnings gap between men and women is narrowing. Women who make it to this level tend to do so on average six years earlier than their male counterparts, though there are still far fewer of them. At all levels, and in most occupations, it's still the case that the average woman earns less than three-quarters of the average man's income for doing the same job.

However, it's interesting that the growth professions (particularly in the Service Sector) tend to be those traditionally thought of as female, while the declining professions (particularly in heavy industry) are traditionally male dominated. If you're contemplating a return to work, but not necessarily to the line of business you were in before, you might like to consider the following table. It shows which occupations are currently enjoying a period of expansion and those which are contracting. We can't guarantee that things won't change. They almost certainly will. But it makes more sense to jump on a band-waggon that's moving along at a fair lick than to join one moving slowly the wrong way along a one-way street!

Expanding occupations

All Professions: e.g. Accountants, Architects, Doctors, Surveyors, Engineers and Scientists of all descriptions.

Technologists and technicians working in the production industries, particularly those related to information technology.

Health Care Occupations: Physiotherapists, Radiologists, etc.

Contracting occupations

Single-skilled craftspeople in industry

Factory operatives

Farm labourers

Unskilled and semi-skilled manual workers

Two fears often expressed by women returners are that they won't be able to cope with the new technology and that they won't have the confidence to put themselves and their opinions forward with sufficient force. If you're contemplating a return to work, here are two questionnaires to help you discover whether you really have anything to worry about. Read each statement carefully, putting a tick in the YES column if you think it is true, and in the NO column if you think it isn't.

	YES	NO
1. When I find myself talking to a telephone answering machine, I usually hang up without leaving a message.	☐	☐
2. I can't help laughing at people who believe that microwave ovens are harmful.	☐	☐
3. I think it's wonderful the way tiny speakers in modern hi-fi systems sound just as good as the big old ones.	☐	☐

4. Whenever I read about a new electronic device for use in the home, I can't wait to try it out. ☐ ☐

5. I'd hate to have to rely on one of those 'hole in-the-wall' cash dispensers if I needed money urgently. ☐ ☐

6. I can't understand why some people have problems getting the right programme taped on their video cassette recorder. ☐ ☐

7. I like these new automatic checkout systems in supermarkets because they reduce the risk of human error. ☐ ☐

8. I've given up trying to find out how to transfer calls on the new telephone system they've installed at work. ☐ ☐

9. Home computers are all very well for the kids, but no one over 30 has a chance of learning how to work them. ☐ ☐

10. Digital watches may suit some people, but I'd never feel easy if I couldn't see the whole watch-face. ☐ ☐

For questions 1, 5, 8, 9, and 10, score 2 points for each YES answer and zero points for every NO. For questions 2, 3, 4, 6 and 7, score 2 points for every NO, and zero for each YES. The higher your score, the more affected you are by technophobia. A score of 14 or more suggests that you are conducting a Canute-like struggle against the tide of technological development. A score of 4 or less implies that you are enviably well-adapted to today's (and probably tomorrow's) world. Most people float in the area between, at ease with those aspects of new technology that they have made an effort to come to terms with, but still suspicious of those outside their experience.

Try this quiz now to see how well you defend your rights. Put a tick in the YES column if you think the statement describes you and in the NO column if it doesn't.

	YES	NO
1. Do you find it difficult to say no to any kind of demand made on you?	☐	☐
2. If someone went to the front of the queue would you do something about it?	☐	☐
3. Do you usually put yourself second in family matters?	☐	☐
4. Do you believe that it is necessary to fight for your rights, otherwise you risk losing them altogether?	☐	☐
5. Do you make a point of complaining if you are sold shoddy goods?	☐	☐
6. Do you have great difficulty in leaving situations when you have had enough?	☐	☐

7. Do you find it difficult to get rid of a salesman who is persistent and wasting your time? ☐ ☐

8. Do you hesitate about asking a stranger directions in the street? ☐ ☐

9. If you were working on a committee would you tend to take charge of things? ☐ ☐

10. If you have been given poor service in a restaurant or hotel, do you always make a fuss? ☐ ☐

For questions 2, 4, 5, 9, and 10, score 2 points for each YES answer, and zero for every No. For questions 1, 3, 6, 7, and 8, score 2 points for each NO and zero for each YES.

The higher your score, the more assertive you are. A score of 14 or more suggests that you have what is sometimes called a strong personality. You insist on other people respecting your rights, and may even be seen as 'pushy'. You certainly won't be seen as a walkover at work, but you might be seen as a bit of a dragon, so remember that assertiveness involves standing up for your legitimate rights, whereas aggression involves trying to deprive other people of their legitimate rights.

A score of 8 or less indicates that you are submissive, a follower rather than a leader, and easily taken advantage of. Watch out, you may be an office dogsbody in the making!

Redundancy

Another group of people who face an interview for a new job with more than usual trepidation are those whose previous job ended abruptly – and often traumatically – in redundancy. Even when it's the result of a scenario which doesn't reflect at all badly on you – a take-over, say – being made redundant is bound to undermine your self-confidence to some extent. And this can make it more difficult for you to present yourself to your best advantage at an interview.

Most redundancy counsellors advise a break to take stock of the situation. They don't recommend spending too much time mourning the job that's gone or feeling sorry for yourself. But they do suggest that you take the opportunity to ask yourself a few fundamental questions. Should you aim to replace the old job with a similar one? Are you absolutely certain that one of the reasons behind your redundancy wasn't the fact that the job didn't really suit you? If a change is what's needed, there'll never be a better time to make it.

Do you really understand why you were made redundant? In real life, it's rarely very clear-cut. Recent research produced some rather unexpected findings about managers who are made redundant. Compared with colleagues who are still employed, they seem to be more intelligent, imaginative, conscientious, and independent-minded. They're also calmer, bolder, less tense and less inhibited. So why on earth are companies dispensing with the services of such paragons of virtue? Well, redundant managers also tend to have some other distinguishing characteristics, and it may be these that make them vulnerable.

For example, they tend to be more trusting, naive and less self-critical than managers who keep their jobs. In other words, they lack survival skills. In organisational terms, they're poor politicians and don't spend enough time cultivating relationships with key colleagues. Redundant managers are described as capable but difficult to get on with and socially inept.

So if you're a redundant manager you should examine your approach to other people. With interviews looming, this is an area you would be looking to polish up anyway. But you need to make sure that you've learnt all the lessons that can be drawn from your recent set-back. Like any other problem in life, you should try to make redundancy work for you rather than against you. And the best way to do this is to draw the right conclusions, take approriate steps to correct any personal weaknesses it has revealed, and then make the most of the opportunity it has created.

If you've been made redundant, make sure that you're fully recovered and hence able to do yourself justice before subjecting yourself to interviews. You must expect interviewers to give you quite a thorough going-over to reassure themselves on this score, so it may be as well to assess two aspects of your personality that may have been badly affected by your recent experience.

The first is self-esteem. If you don't feel good about yourself, you won't find it easy to persuade an interviewer to do so. Answer the following quiz to check this out. Once again, read each statement carefully and put a tick in the TRUE column if it seems to describe you and in the FALSE column if it doesn't.

	TRUE	FALSE
1. I reckon I can do things as well as most people.	☐	☐
2. It's not easy being me.	☐	☐
3. If I had to make a speech, I'd be terrified of making a fool of myself.	☐	☐
4. It's not often that I think of myself as a failure.	☐	☐
5. There are lots of things about myself I'd change if I could.	☐	☐
6. Other people's criticism doesn't often bother me.	☐	☐
7. Other people tend to be better-liked than I am.	☐	☐
8. If I have something to say, I usually go ahead and say it.	☐	☐
9. I rarely feel ashamed of anything I have done.	☐	☐
10. When people say nice things about me, I find it hard to believe they really mean it.	☐	☐

For questions 1, 4, 6, 8, and 9 score 2 points for each TRUE answer; zero for every FALSE. For questions 2, 3, 5, 7 and 10, score 2 points for each FALSE and zero for each TRUE.

The higher your score, the better the opinion you have of yourself. A score of 14 or more suggests that you are quite confident; not necessarily conceited, but you certainly like yourself. A score of 8 or less suggests that you need a bit of psychological stroking, and are probably ready for some changes.

Now that you've reassured yourself on that score, answer the following questions to check that you haven't lost confidence in your ability to control events and to make sure that the things that you want to happen *do* generally happen. Again you must expect interviewers to be alert to the possibility that being made redundant has left you short of optimism. It's this optimism that gives successful managers the confidence to start the new projects that keep a company moving forward.

	YES	NO
1. Is there some habit, such as smoking, that you would like to break but cannot?	☐	☐
2. Do you take steps to control your figure by exercise and diet?	☐	☐
3. Do you believe your own personality was laid down firmly by childhood experiences, so that there is nothing you can do to change it?	☐	☐

4. Do you make your own decisions regardless of what other people say? ☐ ☐

5. Do you find it a waste of time planning ahead because in the end something always turns up causing you to change plans? ☐ ☐

6. If something goes wrong, do you usually reckon it's your fault rather than just bad luck? ☐ ☐

7. Are most of the things you do designed to please other people? ☐ ☐

8. Do you often feel you are the victim of outside forces you cannot control? ☐ ☐

9. Do you usually manage to resist being persuaded by other people's arguments? ☐ ☐

10. Do you laugh at people who read horoscopes to find out what they ought to do? ☐ ☐

For questions 2, 4, 6, 9 and 10, score 2 points for each YES answer and zero for every NO. For questions 1, 3, 5, 7 and 8, score 2 points for each NO and zero for each YES.

The higher your score, the more in control of your life you are. A score of 14 or more suggests you have a healthy degree of autonomy, while a score of 10 or less implies you should be taking steps to get a firmer grip on things.

Internal interviews

Most of the advice you get about the art of being interviewed assumes that the person interviewing you is a complete stranger. But this may not be the case. It almost never is when you're going for a better job in your own company – or when you're undergoing the kind of regular assessment interview that more and more companies now use to check the welfare and progress of their employees.

Perhaps you don't see how there could be any problem about being interviewed by someone you know – and who knows you. Surely you can just talk to them in the usual way, as you have done many times in work meetings or even at social gatherings? This is exactly what you must not do. An interview is a special kind of situation. It's formalised and if it is to be successful, it must be governed by rules and conventions which are very different from those which apply in ordinary conversations – even when the same pair of people are involved.

One of these rules states that the parties involved in an interview must be allowed to perform certain roles. The interviewer must be permitted to start the ball rolling and ask the questions – at least to begin with. The person being interviewed must answer respectfully and show deference to the interviewer's superior status. It's an artificial situation, and it may feel uncomfortable when you know each other. But if either breaks the conventions, by being overfamiliar or suggesting that the situation is ridiculous, the interview will not be successful – for either party.

You should prepare for a promotion interview in your

own company with the same thoroughness you would employ for an interview anywhere else. There's even less excuse than usual for not having researched the background to the post or for being naive or insufficiently penetrating when it comes to your turn to ask the questions. Even when you've been tipped the wink, or given to understand that the interview is a mere formality, don't take any chances. Not everyone on the panel may share that view. Some of them may be backing other internal candidates or perhaps the politics of the situation may have changed in a way you don't know about.

Take your lead from the interviewer(s) in exactly the ways you would if you had never met them before. It's far safer to err on the side of formality or caution than it is to take risks or to exploit the fact that they should already know what a wonderful person you are. Those that hold this view don't need to be reminded. Those that don't – yet – certainly won't be convinced if you don't take seriously an interview they've made time to attend.

Whether you're a new recruit to the job market, or an old-timer with twenty years invaluable experience, you'll need to think about how to handle your new job. In the next chapter we'll be looking at ways of preparing for the big day, and ways of coping with the first few weeks in your new role.

CHAPTER SEVEN
CROSSING THE FINISHING LINE

Let's suppose that you've followed all the good advice in the last six chapters, and you've got yourself a job that sounds just right for you. What happens next?

The company may have 'phoned up with a job offer, or a letter may have landed on your doormat. Your next move should be to confirm that you would like to take up the offer – **in writing**. If the company is really on the ball, they will have sent you your full contract of employment along with the offer letter. Read the contract carefully before you sign it. Check that critical details like the salary and holiday entitlement are mentioned. Read through your responsibilities carefully too. And if there's anything you don't understand, don't be afraid to ring the Personnel Department and ask for an explanation.

Your new employers may ask you to attend a medical before you start. People often get very worked up about the prospect of a company medical examination. In reality, unless you're going for a job as a Physical Training Instructor, or part of a Mountain Rescue Team, it will probably be no more than a rubber-stamping exercise. The most important thing to remember is, don't lie -honesty is definitely the best policy. If you have a physical condition which seriously affects your ability to do the job in question, it is very unlikely not to have emerged at the interview stage.

If you are already in employment, be careful to give your old employers advance warning of your intention to leave. And that doesn't mean telling them on Friday that you won't be back in on Monday! You are required by law to give a certain amount of notice, depending on how long you have been in the job. It should say in your contract how long this period is for you. And really you should have checked this out before even going for interviews so that you could negotiate realistic starting dates with potential employers. The average notice required is one month, though one week is not uncommon.

Preparing yourself

While you're serving your notice, or, if you're unemployed at the moment, while you're waiting to start your new job, there are a number of tasks you should be carrying out in preparation for Day One.

First of all, think about clothes again. If you're going to a similar type of job to the one you already have, you may already have the correct 'uniform' for your new post. All that may be required is a trip to the dry cleaners and a lick of polish on the shoes. However, if you're moving into a completely new line of work, chances are you'll need to rethink your wardrobe.

Your first step should be to make sure that you know what the required dress sense is in your new job. It's better to ring the Personnel Department and ask than to go out and buy three expensive suits only to find that everyone dresses in jeans and jumpers!

If you do have to be smart, making your pennies stretch can be quite a headache. But you don't have to go out and spend a fortune to get yourself kitted up. Look at the suitable clothes you have already, and buy new things which match them. Buy shirts you can wear with both of your suits, or a jacket that goes with both your smart skirts.

No matter what you wear on your first day, it's important that you feel confident in it. Try everything on a few days before the big day – 8 o'clock on Monday morning will be too late for you to go out and buy a tie that matches your suit, or a pair of tights without a ladder in them.

Now's also the time to check that your finances are in order. Explain to the bank manager that you are starting a new job, and that you may need a little financial help bridging the gap between jobs. Check that you know your bank account number and your branch's sorting code, as you'll probably be asked for these on your first day.

A few days before you start, check the times of the local buses or trains and plan your journey to work. Be generous in your estimates and leave time for emergencies like buses breaking down and traffic lights being out of order. If you're really not sure how long your journey should take, do a dummy run at around the same time in the day. It's worth the effort. Arriving late on your first day won't give a very good impression.

You may want to do a little extra preparatory reading

before you start your new job. At the very least, you should read over the company reports and brochures you picked up before your interview. And if you're really on the ball, you'll research the company in much more detail. Ask the Personnel Department for more detailed 'bumf' about the job and about the company's development and performance. You will feel much more confident about your new job if you go in armed with an impressive list of facts and figures.

Action checklist

The night before Day One, think about what you should take along with you the next day. Your employer may have asked you to bring along your P45 (a form which states your personal tax code) and your bank account number and sorting code. He may also ask you for the name and address of your family doctor. Make sure that you take along everything you might need.

Use this checklist to make sure that you're ready for action.

- Are my clothes clean, ironed and ready to wear?
- Are my shoes polished?
- Do I know the times of the buses/trains into work?
- Have I set my alarm clock?
- Have I got my P45?
- Do I have details of my bank account number and sorting code with me?

- Do I know the name and address of my family doctor?

- Is there anything else I should take along?

- Do I know where to report when I arrive tomorrow?

You should now be all set for the launch of the next step in your career. During your first few weeks in your new job, you'll be faced with two challenges. The first is getting to grips with the tasks and responsiblities that go with your job. And the second is getting to know your boss and your colleagues.

Everyone finds new jobs a bit difficult at first. Everything seems so new. And just as you've grasped one bit of information, something else comes up which requires even more thought. Many companies have a reasonably well planned induction programme which is designed to stagger the amount of new information you have to cope with over the first few weeks or months. If you've joined one of them you'll probably find that the main challenge of your first few weeks in a new job is meeting and learning to deal with your new boss and colleagues.

You and your colleagues

It's all too easy to get off on the wrong foot with your new colleagues. Shyness may be interpreted as snobbery, or vivaciousness as insensitivity. Colleagues can make life pretty unpleasant for a new recruit who in their eyes fails to make the grade.

The best way to deal with this kind of situation is to be open and friendly. Ask your colleagues about themselves and try to find common interests. Be patient, and as they get to know you better they'll become less suspicious. And if all this fails, don't despair. An enterprising group of social psychologists have come up with nine rules for getting on with your colleagues. They run as follows:

1. Accept your fair share of the workload. Don't try to shirk out of all the menial tasks, someone has to do them, so make sure you know when it's your turn to make the coffee.

2. Don't criticise your fellow employees in front of superiors. No-one likes sneaks. And you could find yourself on the end of some similar treatment if you don't watch out.

3. Don't be selfish with regard to the working conditions. In other words, don't shout at the top of your voice when people are trying to work. And don't insist on dimming the lights just because you have a headache.

4. Be willing to help if you're asked to. Don't just say you're too busy. You may need someone to help you one day.

5. Try to swallow any personal animosity you may feel towards one of your colleagues. Don't let it interfere with the way you interact with them on a business level..

6. Use your colleagues' first names when you're talking with them. Very few organisations these days use the formal 'Mr' or 'Mrs/Miss' form of address.

7. Ask for help and advice when you need it. People like to be needed. And it's better to ask for help than to make a mistake.

8. Don't be nosey. Let other people's private lives remain just that – private. And don't gossip.

9. Stand up for your colleagues if they are being bad-mouthed behind their back. Your loyalty will not go unnoticed.

If you follow all these rules, handling your new colleagues should present you with few problems. Sometimes though, a problem arises with a particular colleague which seems to frustrate all your efforts to solve it. This may be due to a 'personality clash', where people are just so dissimilar, or even, so alike, that being in the same room seems unbearable. It's often very difficult to know how to deal with this kind of situation. Once again, though, psychologists have looked at the problem and asked people how they would manage a personality clash at work. The suggestions they came up with could prove very useful if you find yourself involved in one of these stormy relationships.

1. Respect each other's privacy. Keep the conversation strictly at a work level.

2. Work hard at being fair towards each other. Examine your motives very carefully after every dealing you have with your colleague. Were they strictly honourable?

3. Don't criticise the other behind their back. It will get back to them, and it will cause a great deal of

resentment.

4. Don't gossip about something your colleague said to you in confidence.

5. Don't feel you have the right to take up other people's free time. Show that you are aware of their time schedules and deadlines and that you respect them.

6. Don't send the other person to Coventry. Ignoring someone you don't like can put a strain not only on you but on most of the office who witnesss it.

7. Repay debts, favours and compliments, no matter how small. You just can't afford to forget about the time she stood in for you at that meeting at the last minute because you slept in. If you do, you can be sure of one thing – she won't do it again!

8. Maintain careful eye contact with the other person during conversation. As we mentioned earlier, poor eye contact conveys the message that you dislike the individual you are talking to, or that you are telling a lie.

9. Don't pretend to like someone when it's blatantly obvious that you don't. No one likes a hypocrite.

Try to get to know colleagues a bit better. First impressions can be deceptive, and you may find that they are not so bad after all. Don't avoid each other. The more you know about what the other is up to, the less hostility and suspicion will be aroused. Finally, be aware of your own personality – especially those aspects of it that may have got you into trouble in the past. Are you intolerant of certain characteristics in others? Are you quick to jump to conclusions? Do you lose your temper with the slightest provocation? Try not to let your personal failings sour your relationship with any of your colleagues.

You and your boss

Of course the most significant relationship you will have at work is likely to be the one with your boss. And they can present their own management problems. Of all the things that people complain about, grumpy, unreasonable and downright rude bosses come top of the list.

The difficult boss comes in many different varieties. And the first step towards coping with them is learning to understand them. And it's not just their behaviour that you need to learn to interpret. What your boss says and what they actually mean may not add up. To keep one step ahead, master the art of mind-reading and discover what your boss is really after.

Here's a brief Dictionary of 'Boss-speak'. See how good you are at translating what they say into ordinary language.

What your boss says	*What they really mean*
'Thank you for your contribution'	'You've said enough for now, so shut up!'
'Can you shed any light on this?'	'I want you to get me out of this mess'

'What's your workload like at the moment?'	'I'm going to pile this lot on you, whether you like it or not'
'We need a meeting about this'	'I need some ideas, and fast'
'I know you'll make the decision'	'I don't know what I'm talking about here so you'd better handle it'
'I know you're the only person who can handle this'	'There's a disgruntled client on the telephone, and I can't be bothered to deal with him'
'I don't mean to be critical'	'I DO mean to be critical'
'This is a rather grey area'	'I'm clueless'
'Just one tiny thing before you go . . .'	'Hope you don't mind missing Eastenders/getting a later train/cancelling your date . . .'

Let's have a look at your boss's behaviour in a bit more detail. Are they usually rotten to absolutely everybody in the office? If so, examine the possibility that they're feeling threatened and insecure at the moment, either because of problems in their private life, or – more likely – because they aren't performing well at work. Try to give them support by praising their work and letting them know that you think they're doing a good job. You don't want to be seen as too much of a crawler, but you should remember that

146

no-one's too grand not to be grateful for some appreciation.

What if your boss is sweetness and light to everyone else in the office and a snarling devil with you? Is this a recent development? Can you link it to something you did recently, or something you failed to do? It could be that some of your little habits irritate your boss. For example, do you always call him 'Sir' when he's told you a million times that just 'Bob' would suit him fine?

Another possible reason for your boss's irritation could be to do with your work. Perhaps he's been disatisfied with your performance lately? Ask your colleagues if they've picked up any hints from the boss. And if all else fails, corner the boss and say that you know they're displeased with your work lately, but you're not sure which bit of it is causing the problem.

It could be that your **methods** of working annoy your boss. Do you spend a lot of time gossiping with your colleagues? Do you pop into the boss's office at five minute intervals to ask questions you should already have the answers to? Do you keep your boss as well informed as you should? Think about the occasions when they've lost their temper with you. Can you spot any pattern to their outbursts? If you can, try and modify your behaviour appropriately.

Of course it could just be that your boss is an unreasonable and bad tempered individual by nature. If this is the case, you'll have to enlist the help and support of your colleagues if you're to make any headway with them at all.

Here are some hints for dealing with the difficult boss:

1. Make sure you know what they want. If his orders are unclear, don't be afraid to ask for clarification.

2. Don't pester your boss unnecessarily. Use your initiative wherever possible.

3. Be willing to accept criticism. Ask your boss not only to point out the problems in your performance, but to outline solutions as well.

4. Put forward your own ideas, and be prepared to defend them if necessary.

5. Don't complain about your boss's behaviour in front of colleagues or superiors. And on no account go to the boss's superior without trying to sort the problem out with your boss first.

6. Be good natured and willing to lend a hand. Even the toughest of bosses will fall for a dazzling smile once in a while.

7. Be ready to express appreciation, but don't grovel. Crawlers are always unpopular.

8. Do what your superior asks you to do. This doesn't mean that you have to be unquestioningly obedient, but it does mean that you have to respect their authority over you.

Stress defusers

One of the real problems that difficulties with your

colleagues or your boss can lead to is work stress. There are also plenty of other things that can lead to stress. Having too much or too little work to do can be very stressful. So can having little or no control over the way you carry out your job. If you play absolutely no part in the decision making process, you begin to feel rather like a pawn in the organisational game.

Another common cause of stress is 'role ambiguity'. If you're not sure exactly what you are meant to achieve in your job, and what your colleagues expect of you, you are likely to feel lost, anxious and unsure. Finally, if your boss demands one thing from you, and your colleagues another, you're likely to feel torn between pleasing your superior, and keeping your friends happy.

What can you do about stress? Well the first step to dealing with it is recognising it in the first place. Try this quiz to see if you are suffering from stress. Read each statement carefully and put a tick in the YES column if the statement seems to describe you, and in the NO column if it doesn't.

	YES	NO
1. Do you often feel you want to burst into tears?	☐	☐
2. Do you bite your nails or have any nervous tics?	☐	☐
3. Do you find it hard to concentrate and make decisions?	☐	☐

4. Do you often feel irritable, snappy □ □
and unsociable?

5. Do you often find yourself eating □ □
when you're not hungry?

6. Do you sometimes feel you're going □ □
to explode?

7. Do you regularly drink or smoke to □ □
calm your nerves?

8. Do you sleep badly? □ □

9. Have you lost interest in sex? □ □

10. Do you feel increasingly gloomy and □ □
suspicious of others?

Analysing your score on this quiz is very straightforward. If you answered YES to more than four of the questions, you should take active steps to reduce the stress in your life.

Unfortunately there are no magic cures to stress. There are some effective coping strategies however. You'll have to experiment with some of the different strategies below to see which ones work best for you.

1. Take action. Try to identify the cause (or causes) of your stress and decide on a plan for tackling them. You'll feel better almost immediately, just because you're in control and doing something about the problem.

2. Practise some sort of relaxation exercise like the

one we outlined in Chapter 3. If you can take some time out each day to take a breath and gather your strength, you'll really feel the difference since relaxation reduces the impact of stress on your mental and physical health.

3. Try to think positively. Research shows that optimists, people with a sunny outlook on life, tend to be show more resistance to the ill effects of stress.

4. Take up a sport and watch what you eat. Physical fitness really does offer you some protection against stress. Taking part in some sort of sport at least twice a week, gives you the opportunity to let off steam and makes it easier to relax afterwards.

5. Don't be tempted to throw yourself even more into your job. Overdoing it on the work front is a sure recipe for stress. Try and keep at least two evenings a week free to do something you enjoy.

6. Practise good time management. Try to get into a routine in the office. Set aside the first hour in every day, for example, to deal with incoming mail. That way you won't end up faced with a huge pile of correspondence needing your attention last thing on Friday afternoons. Make sure that you do your most difficult tasks when you're at your best. If you're a night owl, and you don't come alive until four in the afternoon, don't try to put that new document together first thing in the morning. But above all, don't procrastinate. If something needs doing now – now is when you should do it!

CONCLUSION
THE RIGHT FORMULA

It may seem strange that the last chapter in a book about interviewing has been about what happens *after* a successful interview. We feel this is right because it puts the business of being interviewed into perspective. We see interviews as no more than a means to an end – a passport to the sort of job which offers you what you want out of work and allows you to live life on your own terms. Jobs *are* important, which is why you have to learn to be good at interviews. But there's more to life than work. You need to achieve a balance between your job and other aspects of living. To find out whether you've got the balance right, *try* this final quiz. And if this suggests that your present job has taken over your life, it may be time for a change. If that is the case, we suggest you take a look at the companion guide to this book, The Right Job For You, where we have discussed how you can identify the job which best suits your qualifications, personality and career aims.

	TRUE	FALSE
1. I often go through an entire weekend without spending any time on work brought home from the office.	☐	☐
2. Events at work sometimes force me to miss occasions at home which my family have particularly asked me to get back for.	☐	☐
3. I often dream about work problems.	☐	☐
4. I have at least three significant leisure interests that have nothing to do with my work.	☐	☐
5. When I am ill, I tend to take work to bed with me.	☐	☐
6. I find it easier to talk to work colleagues than to my partner or friends.	☐	☐
7. It is very unusual for me to ring home to say I'm going to be back later than planned.	☐	☐
8. I have had to cancel at least one holiday due to pressure at work.	☐	☐
9. When I'm trying to read a book or magazine, I find that my mind keeps wandering back to work problems.	☐	☐

10. I find it a relief to meet new people ☐ ☐
    who have nothing whatever to do
    with my line of business.

Score your answers as follows. For numbers 1, 4, 7 and 10, give yourself 2 points for each TRUE box you have ticked, and zero points for every FALSE response. For numbers 2, 3, 5, 6, 8 and 9, score 2 points for each FALSE reply, and zero points for every TRUE.

A score of 16 or more suggest that you have managed to achieve a healthy balance between your professional and private life. It's not that you are not fully committed to your job, just that you recognise that professional success does not have to be at the expense of other areas of life.

A score of 12-14 suggests that when office and domestic or leisure interests come into conflict, work comes first. Improving your performance in the office would reduce the number of occasions when you feel forced to disappoint your family and friends.

A score of 10 or less, points to workaholism. For you, life outside the office hardly counts. This is a frame of mind which can threaten your well-being and the happiness of those who care for you. One way to counter this imbalance is by finding ways to make time for yourself away from work.

Training For Your Next Career
Margaret Korving

More and more people are choosing to change careers in mid-stream or perhaps, are forced to make a change due to redundancy. In this timely guide Margaret Korving shows you how to revolutionise your working life. She explains simply and clearly the choices open to you, the range of courses, variety of teaching methods and the cost of retraining.

It includes:
- Combining work with study
- On the job training and government schemes
- Studying from home
- Getting a degree
- Technician, craft, commercial professional courses

Your Green Career

Helen D'Arcy and Gillian Sharp

Can you stay green and still have a financially rewarding job? The authors of this book show you how. It is packed with practical advice on training, pay and job opportunities. It includes interviews with people working in "green" jobs across the country and shows you how to turn your talents into a green career.

It includes:
- Healthy Alternatives
- Food For Thought
- Tilling The Soil
- All Creatures Great and Small
- The Great Outdoors
- National Heritage
- New Scientist
- Quality Control
- Building The Future

Fresh Start
Your Guide To Changing Careers By Men and Women Who Have Done It.
Dennis Barker

The symptoms are all too familiar. Lethargy, depression, inability to concentrate or cope with the daily grind at work. But, don't despair. It is possible to revitalise your life, reassess your priorities and rediscover that elusive job satisfaction. Dennis Barker, author and journalist, has talked to many people who have revolutionised their lives by the simple step of changing their careers. In this book they share their experiences and give positive guidance to others who may be contemplating a fresh start of their own.

It includes:
- Warning Signs
- Family Pressures Trap
- Paths to Giving
- Back to School
- Financial Step-down
- Resisting Ill Luck

All titles available at bookshops. If you have any problem getting the book you require, please contact the publishers Rosters Ltd at 23 Welbeck St, London W1M 7PG. Tel: 071-935 4550.